# FOR THE
# LOVE OF MIKE
### *The Michael MacIntosh Story*

## Sherwood Eliot Wirt

**Oasis International Communications**
**San Diego, California**

Published in Nashville, Tennessee, by Thomas Nelson,
Inc., and distributed in Canada by Lawson Falle, Ltd.,
Cambridge, Ontario.

Printed in the United States of America.

Unless otherwise marked, Scripture quotations are from the
NEW KING JAMES VERSION. Copyright © 1979, 1980, 1982, Thomas
Nelson, Inc., Publishers.
Scripture quotations marked NIV are from the Holy Bible:
New International Version. Copyright © 1978 by the New York Interna-
tional Bible Society. Used by permission of Zondervan Bible Publishers.

Library of Congress Cataloging in Publication Data

Wirt, Sherwood Eliot.
    For the love of Mike.

    1. MacIntosh, Mike, 1944–     . 2. Converts—United States—Biogra-
phy. 3. Evangelists—United States—Biography. I. Title.
BV4935.M23W57    1984          269'.2'0924[B]              84-1140
ISBN 0-8407-5908-8

4 5 6 7 8 9 10 11 - 97 96 95 94 93 92 91

# CONTENTS

# FOREWORD

It has been my pleasure to meet and visit with Michael MacIntosh and to learn something of his commitment to Jesus Christ and his heart for evangelism. He was one of the instructors at our International Conference for Itinerant Evangelists in Amsterdam in 1983. Mike is part of a new generation. Unless our Lord decrees otherwise, he will be one of those chosen to carry the proclamation of the gospel into the twenty-first century. What an honor that will be!

This astonishing story of Mike's life, as narrated by my longtime friend and colleague Sherwood Wirt, speaks for itself. It not only shows human nature at its lowest and highest potential but also provides a message of hope to those whose lives have been marred and twisted by the underside of modern culture. I commend it to its readers and hope that many will find in this book the key to eternal life.

Billy Graham

# ACKNOWLEDGMENTS

Many people have assisted generously in the preparation of this book. I would like to thank particularly Pastor Chuck Smith of Calvary Chapel, Costa Mesa, California; Pastor Edward T. Smith of Calvary Chapel, Encinitas, California; members of the MacIntosh and Riddet families; Robert and Jennie Gillespie, editors of *Horizon International* magazine; Steven Keeling; Don Abshere; Patty Appel; Lee Roddy; Dr. Billy Graham, for his gracious foreword; my wife, Winola Wells Wirt, for unfailing support; and editors Peter E. Gillquist and Larry Weeden of Thomas Nelson, Inc. for wise counsel. I wish to acknowledge the use of a quotation on pages 95 and 96 by the Rev. Chuck Smith taken from Hugh Steven's book, *The Reproducers* (Regal Books, 1972). Certain names in the narrative have been altered to protect living persons.

S.E.W.

# PREFACE

Flipping around the television channels during the holiday season of 1978, I glimpsed a young man sitting on an ottoman in front of a Christmas tree. He was surrounded by children and unopened gift packages and was talking about Jesus. With my thumb on the remote control ready to switch lanes, I paused and waited for the pitch. It never came. I waited for the giveaway. It never came. I looked for the showman's touch, the ego feathers, the bright, lambent smile, the disturbing evidence that religion is just humanity's roundabout way of serving itself. Instead I was drawn by the simple charm of an earnest young man who seemed concerned about ordinary people. From the way he spoke, he understood what a lot of young families were going through. After a while he passed around the packages to his children.

On a Sunday morning not long after, my wife, Winola, and I paid a visit to the old North Park theater on University Avenue in San Diego to hear Michael MacIntosh preach. What we saw and heard, we liked. We realized that God had endowed him with unusual gifts. As we became better acquainted, we also learned that instead of building up his congregation to mammoth size, he had deliberately sent his associates and church members out to start other congregations in the county, many of which were now flourishing. This was different. This broke the pattern. Instead of creating an empire, MacIntosh was dismantling it. I had to find out more.

What I gleaned is the substance of this book. It is a true narrative. Michael MacIntosh and his friends in the ministry are symbols, I believe, of a dramatic change taking place in American church life—a change of which the church itself is only dimly aware. But he is also in his own right a remarkable trophy of grace. Disraeli once cautioned us to read no history, only biography. Words cannot capture a life, but they can make a good story. I commend this one to you.

Sherwood Eliot Wirt
Poway, California
August 1984

# 1

# The Dawn Cracked

*Which way I fly is Hell; myself am Hell.*
John Milton, *Paradise Lost*

*Ram.*

Michael Kirk MacIntosh modulated his voice as the guru had taught him, chanting the sacred word slowly, letting its sound reverberate across the desert floor while he sat and stared at the ghostly outlines of Yucca Valley.

*Ram...Ram...Ram...*

It was four o'clock in the morning and he was hallucinating. The LSD had taken hold; cosmic music was flooding his brain. He was waiting for a flying saucer to appear.

*Ram.*

Below the knoll on which he kept his solitary vigil, Michael could make out the dark shapes of cacti and Joshua trees. The desert night was crisp, the sky was clear, and the full moon was still high. The gist of his meditation in this excellent spot was, "Here I am, stoned and lonely, and living in hell on this stupid mountain."

*Ram.*

Some distance away in a 1967 Volkswagen camper were two spaced-out lovers, Rick and Lori, friends who had driven him out from the city. Down below, gathered around the fence that surrounded a well-lit, white-domed structure, were some of the others. They had assured Michael the building housed a cyclotron, or space machine, that gave off electromagnetic impulses and would take him back in time. Around the edge of the hill stretched an airport where a UFO was supposed to be coming in anytime. Michael leaned back and looked at the stars. They were wobbling. It seemed to him he was gazing at them through the glass of an agitated aquarium. A droning pitch continued to penetrate the silence. It was, he decided, the sound of the cosmos, holding everything together.

*Ram...Ram...*

Disgusted, he quit his chanting. The emptiness of his life had caught up with him. He had torpedoed his marriage. Sandra, his wife, had taken their two-year-old daughter and moved back to Philadelphia and her parents. Michael pictured adorable little Mindi as he had last seen her. He remembered the pink dress with white ruffles, the embroidered sox and white shoes, the curly yellow hair. She was standing by the car in front of the house and waving as he drove off with all his goods, while Sandra stood by the gate looking daggers and hand grenades at him. *God*, he thought, *what have I done?*

Shaking the image out of his mind, he shifted to other dreary subjects. He was thousands of dollars in debt. He had a fistful of traffic citations. His boss, a Santa Ana auto dealer, was unhappy. His draft board was looking for him. There was no end to it! The year was 1969. He was twenty-four years old, and he was living in a roach-infested shack at the end of Twenty-fourth Street near the shore of Newport Beach.

To the east, a faint lightening of the sky appeared on the horizon. Michael watched in a blur as the miracle of a new day brought a subtle change to the desert atmosphere. Somewhere a meadowlark was singing. But now a sharp sound cleaved the air, like the crack of a bullwhip. He looked around but could see nothing unusual, only the first rays of the sun as they spilled down from the mountains and tinted the sagebrush. "I know," he whispered, "it's the crack of dawn. And I've heard it! Me, a social derelict, stoned out of my mind, and I've heard the dawn crack." He watched the streaks in the eastern sky and the changing hues of the desert until, with a final burst of orange, the daylight took over. It seemed to Michael almost as if the universe had exploded. It was the first of many explosions that would punctuate the young man's career.

The leader of the cult that wooed flying saucers was a glassy-eyed drug pusher named Ron, who practiced yoga, Zen, and Satan worship in a run-down section of Orange County. Ron considered himself a messiah. Michael, intrigued by the exciting prospect of contact with outer space, had wanted to meet Ron and was rewarded by the invitation to Yucca Valley and, three weeks later, by Rick's gift of LSD laced with strychnine. After swallowing the capsule in Rick's camper, Michael asked to be dropped off at Ron's hangout, a one-story, brown-shingled shack furnished with discarded junk and perched on the edge of a canyon. Here the faithful came to pick up their acid. Michael found Ron, who seemed distant and preoccupied. Not knowing any of the others present, he sat down to watch television.

It was not long before Michael lost all touch with reality. His vision blurred; his speech became tangled. Ron had become to him a hit man assigned by the Mafia to murder him. The prospect of a violent death terrified him. Michael staggered to his feet and went to find Ron, who was sitting on the floor in the kitchen loading a pistol while his Manson-type followers stood around watching.

Eager to get out of the place, but realizing he was in no shape to do so, Michael said, "Ron, I've OD'd."

Ron looked up. He observed Michael's eyes, the dilated pupils and bloodshot whites. "You're O.K.," he said curtly, shoving a bullet into the chamber. "Just take it easy. No problem."

Michael panicked, "No! Help me. It's a bummer! I'm going numb. My brains are frying. I'm not going to make it. You've got to get me to Hoag Hospital."

Ron stood up and shoved the pistol under his belt. "No way. Cool it!"

But Michael was now yelling. "I'm going to die! I'm going to be murdered in the next few minutes. It's all over. God, help me!" He collapsed in a chair. At a sign from Ron, those in the room began to lay hands on him. They removed his shirt, his shoes and sox, leaving him only his Levis, from which they lifted his wallet. Then they tied his hands behind him and placed a bag over his head. They left him sprawled on a davenport. In the kitchen a tape was playing a Rolling Stones number. *Now I'm really in hell*, thought Michael. *God, do you hear me? I'm in hell!*

Sitting in the darkness, he sensed that spirit forms were hovering around him. It seemed he could make out a likeness of the guru Maharishi, whose teachings he had studied along with those of Edward Cayce and Jeane Dixon. Now the semblance of the Los Angeles metaphysician, Paramahansa Yogananda, was floating about, and Krishna, and the Buddha himself. He called to them: "Help me. I'm not ready to die! Please get me to God!"

They mocked him and cackled, "This is as far as we take man!"

Michael would not be put off. "Take me to God!" he screamed. "I've lost my mind, my job, my wife, my child, my money, but I've paid. I gave 135 bucks to the Maharishi. You take me to God!"

Desperate, and certain that death lay before him, Michael began searching his soul and confessing his sins as fast as he could name them. "I'm a drunk. I'm a liar. I'm a thief. I've lost my wife. I'm taking drugs. I can't face my problems. There's no good in my life. I found it with Sandy but never recognized it. I've failed in everything I ever tried." But somehow it all seemed too late; he was doomed. Nobody could help him, nobody.

With the bag still tied over his head and his arms lashed, Michael bumped his way into a bedroom. He knelt down, pressed his forehead against the floor, and tried to pray. Instead he felt something go up against the side of his head. It may have been Ron's revolver; he never knew. But suddenly he heard a tremendous explosion, so loud he thought it must be a nuclear blast. In his mind's eye he saw a huge ball of fire and flames shooting up into a mushroom cloud. It seemed he was standing in a valley watching it and thinking that he ought to tell people to turn to God before it was too late. He dared not touch his head; he was certain a huge cavity was there and half his brain had been shot away.

Late that evening Rick showed up and drove Michael back to his own pad, where he woke up his older brother Kent. For the next few days he continued in a state of confusion. The physical and psychological effects of that drug trip were to remain with him for years. He was utterly convinced that his brain had exploded. On the following Sunday afternoon he presented himself at the Laguna Beach police station. He related a wild story about the Beatles, saying they were in town and he was part of their troupe. The officers treated him gently and invited him to take a ride with them. They drove him to the Orange County Medical Center.

It was a beautiful February day in southern California. Mockingbirds were singing and the blossoms were on the peach trees, but for Michael MacIntosh life had lost its beauty. He knew he had touched bottom. The easy charm, the puckish, fun-loving demeanor had failed him. Not often had Michael been reduced to tears—once when his older brother, David, was slammed into a telephone pole and killed; once when he broke up with a high school sweetheart; and once, most agonizingly, when Sandra moved out with little Melinda. But on this Sunday morning, Michael cried because he was in a holding tank, locked in the mental ward of a hospital with some strange-looking characters; and he was not getting out.

# 2

# Break in the Clouds

*If the sun and moon should doubt,*
*They'd immediately go out.*
William Blake, "Auguries of Innocence"

According to an impartial survey (conducted by his mother, Ruth Osborn) Michael Kirk MacIntosh was an extremely handsome baby, all eight pounds, twelve ounces of him. His sea-blue eyes reflected the look of his Pictish ancestors in Scotland, while the infectious smile that showed up early was straight from Ireland by way of his maternal great-grandfather. He made his appearance on March 26, 1944, in the delivery room of the Seventh Day Adventist hospital in Portland, Oregon.

Good looks don't matter much, however, when you are poor. And Michael's folks were working class. His grandfather had been driven out of Scotland by deplorable conditions in the shipbuilding industry, but he found work on the Willamette River yards in Portland. His father was a handsome man who went into electronics, but a taste for drink and a lust for gambling made him considerably less than a perfect husband. As for Ruth, Michael's mother, whose father had died when she was seven months old, all her life she had known struggle. Yet this woman, who had no man to guide her when she was small and too many men to try to please when she grew up, was able to bequeath one priceless gift to her three sons—a sense of humor.

Humor is a lower order of faith. Both deal with the irreconcilabilites and incongruities of life. Ruth could laugh when there was no food or money in the house, and she taught her sons to do the same. (Years later, Michael could stand before thousands of youths and joke easily, saying things like, "Would the car get me there on time? God, get me there on time! I pray, O God, I pray! Jesus, help me! Naw, I'll never make it. Come on, blast you. Move, you clunker!" And they loved it.) Laughter was Ruth Osborn's way out of adversity.

Ruth was the gorgeous, blonde, rebellious daughter of a Bible-quoting widow, Ella Rose Lane. Ruth's grandparents, Samuel and Catherine Lane, escaped from Ireland's famine conditions and came to Canada as immigrants in the mid-nineteenth century. Lane was a carpenter by trade. They soon moved to South Dakota where their son, David, was born. Eventually the elder Lanes settled in Oregon, but their son had caught a vision that led him into the Christian ministry. His pursuit of education was such that he would crawl in the window of the local Carnegie library at night to read the books by candlelight. At age nineteen he enrolled in Bible school and, after being ordained a minister of the Methodist Episcopal church, pastored congregations in North and South Dakota. He married Ella Rose, of Yankee and Irish stock, and they in time became parents of two boys and a girl. Then in 1914, when Ruth was seven months old and her father just twenty-seven years, the Reverend David Lane died suddenly of a burst appendix.

Ella returned to normal school, obtained her certificate, and spent the next several years teaching in one- and two-room schoolhouses in the Dakotas. Like many a God-fearing minister's widow of those days, she prayed to God that one of her two sons, if not both, would follow her husband as a preacher of the gospel; and let there be no doubt that she knew the ways of intercession.

But it was not to be. George, her older son, sought personal fulfillment in the unsanctified precincts of United States Gypsum, turning out wallboard, while the younger died at the age of ten during a visit to his grandparents in Portland. As for little Ruth, her mother had tagged her early to be a foreign missionary by the grace of God. But Ruth soon began to think of many more interesting places to live than the interior of China.

When Ella received a telegram telling of her son's illness, she was teaching in the tiny hamlet of Glover, North Dakota. Taking George and Ruth, who had just turned nine, she boarded a train for Oregon. They arrived in Portland a day after the boy died, and never went back. Eventually Ella remarried and established a home in Portland and, later, in Eugene. As for Ruth, she put up with her mother's gung ho Nazarene variety of Methodism (no lipstick, no jewelry, no movies, no dances) until she reached adolescence, when it all seemed hopelessly out-of-date. Living with a prayer warrior, Ruth found, was not easy when the warrior sprang from the loins of Yankee Puritanism.

At age eighteen Ruth raised the flag of independence, slipped across the Columbia River, and married a soldier. This soldier, who feared neither God nor woman, unfortunately mistook his bride for a target in the combat zone. The young girl endured his abuse for three years, during which they became parents of a son whom she named David—for David Lane, the father she never knew. After divorcing, Ruth let several years elapse before she married again, this time to the personable Wilbur MacIntosh.

But while Wilbur was gentler, the home was not one of his top priorities. Following the birth of two sons, Kent and Michael, this marriage also collapsed. Finally, two years after divorcing Wilbur, Ruth married a machinist named Warren "Ozzie" Osborn in 1950. Michael was now six years old.

Between her second and third marriages to Wilbur and Ozzie, Ruth found work as a receptionist. During weekdays she placed Michael and Kent, then four and five, with a middle-aged German couple named Hofmeister who had a small farm and orchard outside of Portland. The melancholy experience of those two years left its mark on Michael.

First, there were the snakes. The cornfields were full of them, and when Kent started first grade and crossed the field to the bus stop and Michael would walk with him, they invariably encountered half a dozen garter snakes. Once when they were playing, Kent and another boy picked up Michael and tossed him into a haystack. A snake was lying in the stack and bit him in the arm.

Then there was the bedwetting. This was a daily trial not only to Michael but to his proxy mother, who tried everything, including dressing the boy in girl's clothes, to shame him. A coffee can was placed under his bed at night. Then there were the spankings. A ruler applied to the back of the hand was Mrs. Hofmeister's method; her husband worked on the more familiar part of the anatomy. Michael was spanked for not knowing how to tie his shoelaces (Kent had to teach him). He was spanked for running through the rows of corn with the collie dog chasing him and knocking off the ears. He hated the farm because even at that age he knew what love was, and the love of a mother and father wasn't there.

Mrs. Hofmeister was a well-meaning, pious woman, if rather uncommunicative. She taught Michael to read the

Bible and did what she could to provide a home away from home. But the raw milk from her cow transmitted bacteria that produced undulant fever in Michael—an affliction that caused rapid rises in his body temperature for years. As for her husband, he was (in Michael's words) overbearing, bull-headed, and hypocritical. One weekend when the two little boys were at home with their mother, the foster parents drove to the house to pick them up and take them back to the farm. Michael, who was sitting at the table, saw who it was and, leaving his dinner, disappeared out the back door. It was hours before they found him hiding behind a fence.

After her third marriage, Ruth collected all her boys, and she and Ozzie Osborn established a full-time home in a small, two-bedroom frame house. David was by now a high school senior and Michael was six. For the half-dozen years that Ruth and Ozzie lived together, Michael had the only father he was ever to know. They were good years. Ozzie was pleasant to the boys and the family became close. For a while Michael took the surname Osborn as his own. He became active at William Clark Elementary School and joined the Cub Scouts and the school band, taking up the trumpet. As he grew older, he took part in science fairs, acted the role of Captain Corcoran in a production of *H. M. S. Pinafore*, and was elected vice-president of the student body. He made first string on the school basketball team and also played on the YMCA Gra–Y's and the Montavilla Baptist Church team.

There was a sweetness to Michael's nature, his mother said, that made him popular with everyone. In the early school grades he became a leader and an achiever, the head of his class. He would get the whole family involved in the projects he was engaged in, whether it was a science exhibit or making model airplanes. He showed a love for other people and little creatures, and was particularly sympathetic to the misfits and the left-out. If a buddy was having trouble at home, he would bring him to his own house. If a sparrow was lying on the ground with a broken wing, he would carry it home.

The Montavilla church was located across the street from the school, and some of Michael's friends began inviting him to Sunday school. Church had never been a part of Ruth's weekly routine since she left home, but now Michael enjoyed the friendships, the sports, and sitting in church with a red-haired girl named Diane. It seems he had always believed in God, and his reading of the Bible was one pleasant memory from the farm. When he walked in the fields and saw shafts of sunlight breaking through the clouds that so often cover the Oregon skies, he would imagine that angels were walking down them to visit the earth. One Sunday morning some missionaries from Africa came to Montavilla and spoke to the Sunday school children. The man preached a powerful message and gave the children an opportunity to commit their lives to Christ. "Keep your heads bowed and your eyes closed," the missionary said, "and just put up your hand."

Diane, sitting next to Michael, squirmed, and he thought she was raising her hand. Impulsively he raised his. *This means*, he thought, *that we'll go down into the basement and talk, and I'll get to be with her.* But she didn't raise her hand; in fact, Michael was the only one in the room to do so. Now he was forced to examine his motive. What did he want to do? The room was becoming stuffy, and he liked it downstairs; that was where the classrooms were and where he played hide-and-seek. He decided to go, Diane or no Diane. When he reached the basement he found his Sunday school teacher crying.

Michael had never seen a man's tears before. "Why are you crying?" he asked.

"Don't you realize what you've just done?" asked the teacher.

"Well, I raised my hand to say that I believe Jesus is the Son of God."

"But you will have eternal life!" The man believed his pupil had done something more than what Michael thought he had done. But Michael wanted to believe, and his teacher explained the simplicity of the gospel.

Michael knelt on the cold linoleum floor, put his arms on the seat of a gray metal folding chair, and asked God to forgive his sins.

Afterward, while he was walking home, he kept looking up and waiting for the skies to open so he could see God. He told his mother he had become a Christian; and Ruth, who had been through it all with the Methodists and Nazarenes, took it in stride. At school Michael continued to bring home top grades, and he was becoming an outstanding basketball player. What life held for him was still around the bend; but right now the stream was flowing calmly and it all looked good.

# 3

# Powerdive

*He was a hundred thousand feet up, dropping toward the ocean like an enormous cannonball.*
Tom Wolfe, *The Right Stuff*

One day in 1956, Michael came home after basketball practice at William Clark Elementary School to learn that his stepfather, Ozzie, had left, and his mother was filing for divorce. He couldn't believe it. Most of his life was wrapped up in school and Scouting activities, and he had been paying little attention to what was happening at home, but there had never been any intimation of a split. It was as if his world had come apart, and there was nothing he could do about it. To spare Michael as much as possible the pain and shock she knew he would go through during the divorce proceedings, his mother suggested he pay a visit to his older brother David, and she put him on a train for Sacramento.

David MacIntosh had always been the star in Michael's life. David, after graduating from Franklin High School, had studied at Lewis and Clark College and at the University of Oregon; then, realizing he was about to be drafted, he had enlisted in the Air Force. Within a short time he was assigned to the security division and was on his way to the war zone in Korea. After the truce of Panmunjom he moved to California, married a young woman from Sacramento, and went to work for a civilian airline. He and his wife, Liz, became parents of a baby boy.

Michael spent two wonderful weeks in Sacramento, where he was intrigued by the influential friends David seemed to have, both in the military and in civilian life. David knew everybody. He had come home with only the rating of an airman first class, yet he had access to important businessmen and security clearance to Air Force installations where he apparently had continuing connections.

Not as handsome as Michael, nor as tall as his brother would one day be, David managed to combine his mother's ebullient sense of humor with his Grandmother Ella's strong character. He was very close to his grandmother and she thought the world of him.

In Michael's eyes, his older brother symbolized money, power, and influence. He was a bright light in a dark period, the only positive influence in Michael's life, the one successful person in a poor family.

David loved Kent and Michael and took a personal interest in the boys. When they were small, they would sit on his lap and steer his 1940 Ford sedan. As they grew, David took time with them, showed them how to make model airplanes, told them stories, and taught them tricks.

At the time of Michael's visit in 1956 David was enrolled in philosophy courses at Sacramento State College, intent on earning a degree. During those two weeks, David tried to make Michael face reality. He taught him to reach higher, showing him that there is more to life than the circumstances one is raised in. Whatever situation David faced, he seemed to look above it, and in the process he fired Michael's imagination. In one memorable conversation during that Sacramento visit, David challenged Michael to consider the consequences of his dreams:

"What do you have for goals when you grow up, Mike?"

"I dunno. I think maybe I'd like to be a chaplain."

"A chaplain! That will cost you something."

"What do you mean?"

"I mean in discipline and in separation from the world."

It was during that visit Michael learned for the first time that David was actually his half brother, that David's surname was not MacIntosh, and that their mother had been married not twice but three times. This knowledge staggered Michael. He returned home depressed. Life was not the same. The house was empty much of the time. He just couldn't understand why these things were happening to him.

Michael's other brother, Kent, entered Madison High School and became the epitome of vigorous youth. Two inches shorter than Michael but a year older, he established an enviable record in football (defensive back), track (sprints), and wrestling (147-pound class). At one time Kent held the city wrestling championship for his weight, and on another occasion he was voted the most inspirational player on the Madison Senators football team. While the brothers engaged in the usual sibling rivalries, to Michael, Kent was a hero; and when the younger brother reached high school he tried hard to emulate the older, but with less success. Even so, Michael acquitted himself well in Kent's three sports, plus basketball. On one occasion, Ruth was presented with a specially designed award for being the most outstanding mother in Madison High, a school of 2,700 students.

One day in 1959, Michael visited a corner store near his home with a couple of buddies and, for the first time in his life, engaged in shoplifting. It was an insignificant item—a fifteen-cent tube of glue for a model airplane they were putting together. As they came out of the store a pickup truck drew to the curb. Michael recognized Penny Williams, the wife of his brother David's closest friend.

"Get in the truck, Mike," she said.

His heart jumped. How had she found out about the tube of glue? "What's the matter?" he asked.

"Get in, and I'll tell you."

He climbed into the cab and waited nervously for her to say more.

"Your brother David was killed today," she finally said, fighting back the tears.

"That's a lie!" Michael shouted. "Don't ever say anything like that to me again!"

"I'm sorry, but it's true. Your sister-in-law Liz just called me. He was killed in a car accident."

Together they went to the Rose City apartments, a large lower-income complex where Kent and Michael lived with their mother. Ruth was home from work and was tidying up the place. Penny sent Michael into the small kitchen to prepare coffee while she sat down with Ruth. Soon Michael heard a scream such as he had never heard before. "He's dead! He's dead!" Ruth cried as he entered the living room.

Michael reacted coldly, still unable to accept it. "There's nothing we can do about it," he said. But Ruth gripped his arm in her powerful hands and nearly broke it, while she poured out her grief. Later he drove out to the centennial fair where Kent was working and broke the news to his brother.

As the full meaning of the tragedy came home to Michael, it was as if someone pulled the key from his ignition. He just went dead. David was only twenty-six years old, and now he was gone forever. Ruth had no money for the journey to Sacramento, but her fellow employees took up a collection to put new tires on her 1956 Ford Victoria and have the engine tuned. Together the little family made the journey to the funeral. It was summer, and the valley was hot. Michael and his mother visited the funeral home for the viewing; and as he stared at the open casket, he couldn't believe his brother was gone.

The whole thing seemed unreal. A man whom David knew had bought a new car. He showed up before work and invited David to take a ride. David had just signed an insurance policy; it was lying on the table. They went riding out into the open country where there was nothing but farmland. A single telephone pole stood by the road and the car had struck it. The Sacramento *Bee* said the vehicle was traveling seventy miles an hour. David was killed; the driver was critically injured. It took several hours to pry David's body out of the seat.

At the military funeral a guard of honor fired a rifle salute, and the flag that covered the casket was given to Liz. David was buried with his rank of airman first class, but Michael was again impressed by the number of Air Force officers and city officials who had known David and took the time to attend the service.

From the time Michael returned to Portland much of the fun went out of his life. He gradually stopped studying and participating in sports. He ceased to attend the Baptist church. At Madison High he joined the Young Life club and was elected president, but he attended mainly for the socializing and the chance to meet girls; for girls had now become the main pursuit of Michael's life. One Friday evening as he sat in a parked car on a side street with some friends, someone said, "Let's have a beer." Michael had never tasted it, but that was the beginning of his venture into a new lifestyle: parties, drinking, drive-in movies, and girls. They proved poor salve for the open sore left by David's death.

By the time he was sixteen years old Michael had wandered in and out of several high school relationships and had fallen in love with a girl named Anne who lived in the end apartment at the Rose City flats. Anne was two years older than Michael, but he was now six feet tall and desperately infatuated. All he could think of was marriage, but Anne didn't believe he was responsible enough for such a step. Eventually she left town and moved to Eugene, where she enrolled at the University of Oregon. Her departure left Michael desolate. He lost interest in whatever remained to him, dropped out of Madison High in his senior year, and failed to graduate with his class.

With nothing to do, Michael began spending his time with a gang of toughs, getting drunk and engaging in nightly stunts. On one occasion they invaded a hotel notorious for prostitution and ran through the halls, banging on doors. On another, Michael kicked out a window pane in a warehouse and slashed his leg severely, the injury sending him to the hospital. There the leg became infected, and Michael had plenty of time to think. One day while he was lying in the ward, the local Young Life leader came to visit him. It was one of those moments when a life's direction hung in the balance. Michael said to his friend, "Jack, I want to know God. I just can't keep on living like this." Whatever Jack's reply was, the moment passed without Michael's making any moves.

Before he left high school, where he was sports editor of the school paper, his journalism teacher had said to him, "Don't quit. You've got talent. It would be the biggest mistake you ever made." But he made it. He had promised his mother that he would go to night school and finish up, that he would find work and help support the family, but he did nothing. The powerdive from A student to dropout left him completely uncaring and rebellious. He saw no hope and no future. Everything was a heartbreak. Even church seemed to be little more than a set of admonitions—Don't drink! Don't smoke! And as for the rest of the world—he became convinced that nobody ever made it to the top unless he was either rich or a crook.

He thought of Anne constantly. He saw her on occasion (Ruth always drove the family to Eugene to spend holidays with Grandmother Ella), and Michael's passion and eloquence finally broke down the girl's reluctance and overcame her good judgment; she agreed to marry him. But once again, when he faced the prospect of assuming adult responsibility, he could not rise to it. In a dramatic meeting for which he once again fortified himself with alcohol, he told Anne he could not go through with the marriage. She, deeply wounded, told him he would never see her again. Michael said he didn't care—but he did, and he knew it. Three months later, in Army uniform and depressed, he mailed her a letter telling her how sorry he was and asking if they could begin again. She wrote a brief reply, saying she was married.

# 4

# Wham! Wham!

*Stop, children, what's that sound?*
Steven Stills, "For What It's Worth"

*The answer, my friend, is blowing in the wind.*
Bob Dylan, "Blowing in the Wind"

Rebelliousness was in the air. The "free speech" movement had invaded the Berkeley campus of the University
of California. Stickers reading QUESTION AUTHORITY!
were appearing on hotrod bumpers. Voluntary military
enlistments were at low ebb. "Nuts to you!" "Who says
so?" "Why should I?" "Get off my back!" "What right do
you have to order me around?" "Kiss off!" The word was
out: don't trust anyone over thirty. The old boys had their
chance and wasted it. If we can't do much, we can at least
stop them.

Ever since he could remember, authority had presented
a problem to Michael. At the age of four he resented being
told what to do by the Hofmeisters. He was sure these
strangers were the wrong people to direct his life, but he
never did find the right people. His career as a Boy Scout
foundered when an ex-Marine scoutmaster took over the
troop. Michael couldn't take the discipline. Without a fa-

ther, and with a mother working early and late and barely keeping her family together, he did everything he thought he could get away with. As he saw it, the problem was not right and wrong, but sheer, raw power—over him.

Once he dropped out of high school, insubordination became a way of life. If he was told to do something, he would likely do the opposite. Paradoxically, he considered joining the Army "to prove himself," as he liked to think; actually it was to impress Anne. Ruth, who was painfully aware of his lack of discipline, suggested that before he enlisted he might try the National Guard and see whether military life appealed to him. It seemed like a sound idea, even if it did come from his mother. In January 1962 Michael, being seventeen years of age, signed with the Guard and was shortly whisked off to camp.

Military life provided Michael with a new stage for his act and a new audience for his jokes. He taxed his imagination thinking up ways to show he was in charge of himself, such as missing meetings, ignoring the salute, and mouthing off at Guard officers. Once he showed up at morning inspection with a toothbrush in his mouth. At that time six months of regular Army active duty were required of all Guardsmen, and Michael's superiors were happy to cut his orders to Fort Ord, near Monterey, California. All through boot training and later, when the troops engaged in simulated combat exercises, he continued his relentless and frantic clowning.

During war games at Fort Ord, Michael was named one of the "aggressors" who was supposed to try to capture a defending company camped on a hill. The defenders were waiting in foxholes, and the aggressors were ordered to crawl across a couple of miles of woods and open fields. After dark Michael stopped crawling and ran at a crouch. Flares were sent up, a searchlight was turned on, and it only made it easier for him; for now he could see where everybody was. He sneaked past the holes and approached the command post, which was down in a hole and built up with sandbags. Michael crawled on his belly to the entrance, holding his M-1 rifle, and spotted a guard outside the door. Near the front was an observation slit, and he planned to jam his bayonet through it and yell, "You are my prisoners!" Unfortunately he stuck his bayonet into a sandbag and roused the guard. But he got his weapon out before they captured him and announced, "You are my prisoners!" It seems he had singlehandedly captured the colonel, the major, and everyone in the command post. Thus ended the war game.

During some National Guard exercises in the state of Washington he had a similar experience. This time he and some other troops were dropped off in a wood and were supposed to make their way back. Michael, however, climbed in the back of one of the trucks that had deployed them and rode back into camp. Once inside, he jumped out and sneaked through the brush until he found two foxholes and captured them both. He threw in a pinecone and said, "Hey, you guys, you're dead!" After that he walked over and X'd them with chalk in the prescribed manner. It turned out he had captured the commanders and the game was over. To cap it, during duty at Yakima firing range he created a stir by calling headquarters and advising the master sergeant in a muffled voice that "Senator Kennedy and a team of top brass" were on their way to inspect the camp.

Basic training was followed by assignment to an Army administration course. Before reporting for classes each day, the troops were mustered for parade and morning exercises. With a fellow conspirator Michael devised the practice of dropping from the second-floor window of the barracks to the ground and wandering into the PX for coffee and doughnuts. Later they would appear at roll call.

This unauthorized walkout was discovered by a regular Army sergeant who had been a World War II hero. As punishment he ordered Michael and his partner to clean two unused barracks that were being readied for an incoming group of recruits. They accepted their reprimand with a show of humility; but when they examined the barracks and learned the magnitude of their task, they went into conference.

Instead of setting to work with pails and mops, they put on arm bands that made them look like platoon sergeants and sauntered down to the main reception center where the new recruits were arriving. "All right," said Michael, "who's in charge here?"

He was sure he would find some egoistic, macho-type high school kid who would be eager to respond. And of course, one of them did speak up: "What is it, Sarge?"

"I need a detail of twenty men with mops and buckets." They were quickly rounded up. Michael and his buddy then ordered the men into formation and paraded this hilarious Tom Sawyer brigade, with mops at the shoulder, up the main street of Fort Ord, past the PX, the bowling alley, and the military headquarters to the waiting barracks. The cleaning was accomplished in short order; and Michael then advised the men that because of the good deed they had performed for their country, they could take off the rest of the day and do as they wished—go bowling or get drunk at the PX. The decorated sergeant in due course inspected the barracks and found them serviceable, but never did learn who cleaned them.

In all his clashes with Army authority, the question of Michael's patriotism never came up. The Vietnam issue did not trouble him; he hardly knew what it was. Michael was never mad at anybody in particular; the bitterness that made him a rebel without a cause went much deeper. Behind the antics and the heavy drinking was a young man with a broken heart who kept saying to himself, "This world stinks. Life is baloney. Nothing turns out right. What am I doing here and why?"

Ozzie had moved out, Anne was lost forever, David was dead—now what? Depressed by such melancholy thoughts, Michael continued to cover up with comical and erratic behavior as he careened downhill. His active duty with the Army completed, he was sent home, and a year later he received a "general discharge with honorable conditions." That made him once again eligible for the draft, and within days he was summoned to appear before a Portland draft board.

In order to emphasize how unfit he was for further military service, Michael deliberately filled out the draft board's questionnaire with the wrong answers. Did he have dizzy spells? Yes. Upset stomach? Yes. Mental illness? Yes. A lieutenant in the medical corps called him in.

"What is all this?"

"I just don't think I'm fit to be a soldier. I've got the wrong attitude." Michael then described his antics in the National Guard and his hostility toward authority. The lieutenant began asking questions, and David's death was brought up. The lieutenant listened, and decided Michael should be given a year to get over the emotional stress caused by David's accidental death, after which he would again be called up.

Kent meanwhile had begun working in a Portland steel foundry, and Michael, now a free man, applied and was hired. He spent the next twelve months swinging sledgehammers and hoisting one-hundred-pound weights for Esco Steel. For a nineteen-year-old just out of uniform and in superb condition, it was great stuff. The crash of metal, the giant cranes, the pouring of white-hot steel, the pounding of drop forges, the hard hats, the ugly, grimy windows, the very gutsiness of the place appealed to him.

These were not toy soldiers chanting "Onward Christian Soldiers" as they paraded past the post chapel; these were steelworkers, men with rough tongues and bulging muscles, the very foundation of America's work force. The pay was good and Michael reveled in the hard work. He learned to drink whiskey, worked the pinball machines, and lived on cheeseburgers and chili.

The first job to which Michael was assigned was knocking the slag off the chain links when they came out of the furnace. After he had built up some muscle they moved him to what was called the "dog house." Here he would pick up the heavy weights that were sitting on the molds where they poured the steel. After the steel was poured, he moved the mold swiftly to the next one and kept going. He lasted six months—longer than anyone his age, he says, except his brother. He was then transferred to the scrapyard, directing the man in the overhead crane. He would mix up train wheels and different kinds of scrap metal and put them in buckets. Then the crane with its giant magnet would lift them to the pouring place.

Michael was good at the work and enjoyed it. It gave him self-esteem and identity with the men, most of whom were black. It was nothing for each of them who worked in that heat to drink a six-pack of beer at a sitting and smoke a pack of cigarettes and tell a lot of dirty stories— that was the lifestyle. Michael could play a good game of pool and drink any of them under the table. Physically he was stronger than he had ever been in his life.

And yet it kept coming back, the bitterness and frustration, tensing his body each time he swung the hammer. Where is God? *Wham!* Where is my dad? *Wham!* Where is Anne? *Wham!* Where is David? *Wham!*

Later, the snowballing of disappointment would drive him to commit one of the major mistakes of his life. He began dating Jennifer, a girl he had known at Madison

High School. She was sweet, she loved him, and her family consented, reluctantly, to the match. But Michael knew he was treading on perilous ground because he did not love her as he should. One night in early 1964, on impulse, he proposed marriage to her and she accepted. The wedding date was set, but as it approached he became sickeningly aware that he had made a mistake. He appeared at the ceremony late—and intoxicated. Two weeks later he moved out of their apartment, leaving Jennifer desolate. Her family did everything they could to salvage the marriage, but it proved hopeless. Efforts to secure an annulment failed, and six weeks later they were divorced.

"She was a very nice girl," Michael would later say. "I hurt her badly, and I hurt her family. It was totally my fault and I offer no excuse. But then, nothing I did at that time turned out right. Life had molded me into a walking calamity."

# 5

# The Water Can

*He drives like a madman.*
2 Kings 9:20 NIV

It was ten o'clock on a Sunday morning in the fall of 1963. Thousands of Portland Christians were either in church, on their way to church, or at home trying to make up their minds. Meanwhile thousands of other residents of the City of Roses were streaming south on highway 99W heading for the McMinnville drag races—America's new national craze, directly descended from the chariot races that intoxicated ancient Rome.

At the freeway offramp leading to highway 18, a preposterous traffic jam had formed. Green, blue, beige, buff, and raspberry vehicles of every imaginable size and description were bumper to bumper, impatiently idling, engines racing and snorting. Occasionally a supercharged Oldsmobile would roar out of line and cut down the embankment—then horns would honk and a siren would wail. Waiting in the lineup was Dick Zugman, scion of an old Portland family and heir to a cluster of jewelry stores. Dick was tooling a box-shaped little MG that boasted a Corvette engine. He liked to spend his Sundays drag racing, and on this particular day he had lured a friend along.

That friend was Michael, who was idling just behind him in a 1956 two-door Chevy hardtop.

Michael was excited. Thanks to a recent car accident that had left him with a mild whiplash, an insurance company had come through with $1,200. "Bank it," advised his friends, but Michael chose to slap it down on the Chevy. First he adorned his treasure with chrome wheels, then he installed a different engine built up to Corvette specifications. Behind the wheel of this souped-up creation he could forget everything, and Zugman's invitation to race was the neatest thing yet.

As he waited for the traffic to move, Michael noticed his engine was heating up. He raised the hood and found the fan belt had broken. He let the engine cool, but by the time they reached the drag strip he knew he was in big trouble.

The strip itself was a wild intrusion into the placid farm country of the Willamette valley. A flat, open field had been transformed into a blacktop runway a quarter of a mile long. At one end was the starting line, and by it a ten-foot tower was standing on stilts. At the other end was the finish, where electric timers had been rigged. Adjacent to the tower was a paved artery leading off the track to the pit area. Here a hundred cars were coughing and rumbling and belching rings of blue smoke as mechanics in coveralls worked on them. In the middle of the pits were other cars lining up for the next race, with engines roaring. Several hundred people were seated in bleachers alongside the track, and another hundred stood around the starter with his flags.

Of assorted liquids Michael found no lack of supply, but no water for his engine. Half a mile away stood a farmhouse, and there was nothing for it but to start walking. In due time he was back with a full five-gallon water can, borrowed from a good-natured farmer. Michael reasoned that as the drag strip was so short in length, the broken fan belt would not knock him out of the race. He tanked up and drove to the entry area where the drivers were lining up for classification assignments. The official, unaware that Michael's engine was different from the usual stock Chevy, routinely assigned him to the stock class. A registration number was duly painted on his car window.

His race was called, and Michael lined up with one other car for the first heat. At the flag he slammed his engine into low gear, floored the accelerator, and leaped two lengths ahead of his rival before the powerglide shifted into drive. By the end of the quarter mile he was racing at a hundred miles an hour and won easily. Thanks to the farmer's water can he survived two more heats, and the eliminations were completed. As preparations were made for the final run, some friends of an eliminated driver walked over to Michael's Chevy and studied it. They listened to the cam and the solid lifters, and one of them raised the hood.

"Hey!" he shouted to Michael, "you're not a stock." Michael responded by ignoring him and going to the starting line, where he roared out ahead of the remaining contender, as he had done in the heats, and captured the event. Tingling with pride he drove around the back of the strip and approached the tower to receive his trophy. It was a moment never to forget: his first race, and he had come off a winner! He accepted the trophy, smiled for the camera, waved to the applauding crowd in the bleachers, and drove back to pick up some tools and the five-gallon can. As he stepped out of the Chevy he found himself in an ugly crowd, and facing him was the director of the racetrack.

"We want that trophy back."

"You want what?"

"The trophy. You won your race illegally."

"What do you mean? I paid my five dollars. There's my registration number on the window."

"It's your engine, Buster, your engine."

"What about my engine?"

"It's illegal. Give back the trophy and we'll forget it. Otherwise we'll have you kicked out of the National Hotrod Association."

Michael laughed, "I don't belong to the National Hotrod Association."

But now, he noticed, several of the onlookers were making menacing moves and gestures. Turning quickly, he jumped into the Chevy. "Baloney!" he shouted, waving the trophy. "I won this race and it's mine!" And down the road he roared, his radiator leaking a trail in the dirt.

Several of those present leaped for their cars and the chase was on. But they did not reckon on the water can. Michael had promised to return it, and a short distance down the road he swung off (the leak having by this time run out) and drove up a lane leading to the farmhouse. The can was returned after Michael tanked up for the last time, while a string of cars disappeared down the highway. He took his time driving back to Portland.

# 6

# Nowhere Man

*Living in a nowhere land.*
The Beatles, "Nowhere Man"

In 1964 President Johnson was touting the "Great Society" while he shipped hundreds of thousands of draftees to Vietnam. The student protest movement was taking over dormitories and college administration buildings, attacking the ROTC and burning flags. Gasoline was cheap and jobs were not hard to pick up. Jean-clad hitchhikers with bedrolls on their backs dotted the highways. Everyone was listening to Bob Dylan, the new prophet of the streets, and to the incredible Beatles, who had appeared on Ed Sullivan's show and were shaking the earth with their music.

Among those caught up in Beatlemania was twenty-year-old Michael MacIntosh. He quickly learned all the Beatle songs; and when their motion picture *A Hard Day's Night* appeared, he sat in theaters hour after hour, watching, listening, projecting himself into the picture. Fresh out of the divorce court, his mind was stunned, and his soul was frozen by what had happened to him. He found it easy to fantasize amid the crash and jangle of the dusty, cavernous, dimly lit steel foundry. Like hundreds of other young men of the sixties, he dreamed of a lifestyle like that of the Beatles. What they said, he thought. What they did, he wanted to do.

By October he had put in a full year working and had $350 in his pocket. He would go to London and look up the Beatles. He talked another young steelworker into quitting, and together they set out in a 1964 Ford Falcon. They drove first to the San Francisco Bay area, where Anne was now living. Michael had refused to believe she was married and still hoped for a reconciliation. His hopes were soon dashed as he could not find her address. They stopped in Hayward, where his friend went into a bar and Michael entered a telephone booth on the street to call his former roommate in Portland. While he was talking, a small, glassy-eyed man approached the booth. Michael opened the door to tell him he would soon be out, whereupon the man pulled a stiletto and lunged at him. Michael slammed the door on the man's wrist and the knife clattered to the floor. He then began hitting the man on the hand with the receiver while yelling into the mouthpiece for help. The assailant opened the door, collected his weapon, and disappeared before the desired help came from Portland.

The journey continued, the pair taking turns driving, sleeping, and reading the latest James Bond suspense novel, *Goldfinger*. They arrived in Manhattan ready to take on the town, eager to find out what the "truth" was that Bob Dylan was singing about, convinced that like James Bond they could acquit themselves in any situation. After taking lodgings in the Sloane House YMCA, they set out for the Hudson River docks, aiming to work their passage across the Atlantic. The visit proved fruitless, as the union hiring halls had no interest in them. At night they wandered up to Times Square, where transvestites beckoned to them from Forty-second Street doorways, and a badly beaten man with a bloody head staggered out of an alley, begging for help. They stared at the porno shops and bought an astrological chart for fifty cents. The world was indeed an amazing place. In the Peppermint Lounge they ogled the celebrities dancing the "twist," a new dance Chubby Checker had invented and introduced.

One evening, wearing blazers and neckties, they were approached by a black man. "Hey, guys, do you want a little action?"

"What are you talking about?"

"Well, do you want some girls?"

"Well, yeah."

"Follow me then, but don't walk with me."

"Oh, sure." And after looking around furtively, he disappeared around a corner. They followed him. This was the big city! This was life! He took them to the subway, made two changes of trains en route, and they finally ended up in Harlem, surrounded by ugly tenement buildings. After keeping his two customers waiting for a considerable time on a stairway landing, the man returned with two large companions.

"What kind of girls do you want?" one of them asked. "Indian, Mexican, Japanese, or what?"

"Golly, we don't know."

"Well, give us your money. Your wallets, your watch, your rings, all your valuables."

"Why?"

"I hate to tell you, but these girls steal. It's O.K., we'll put it all in an envelope and register it at the desk. You'll get it back."

It sounded odd, even to a naive twenty-year-old from Oregon. Michael gave him a little money and his friend gave him more. The three men then disappeared upstairs, and after a while someone came up from below carrying grocery bags full of liquor. "Where are you going?" asked Michael.

"I'm going upstairs."

He soon came down and Michael commented, "What's it all about? It sounds like a party going on up there."

The man smiled. "You're the party," he said.

A cold feeling crept over Michael as he realized the man was telling the truth. He and his friend went down to the street and saw fifteen or more members of a youth gang approaching them, flashing switchblades. They backed away facing the gang, until they reached the corner, where they turned and ran for their lives. When they reached the subway entrance they saw a policeman walking his beat, wearing his rain slicker. They told him what had happened, how they had been ripped off. Would he go back and get their money for them?

"Hey, Punk," said the officer, "I'm not going to get killed for you."

"But you're a—"

"Get moving."

After three such weeks of the Big Apple's hospitality, and with no chance of getting to Europe, the young men drove back to the West Coast nonstop in two-and-a-half days. Michael's first attempt to get away from Portland had ended in failure.

During the winter of 1964–65 Michael lived by finding odd jobs and writing bad checks. At times he became so depressed he would stay in bed for days, feeling lonely, frightened, and empty. When his money ran out he would wander into restaurants, order meals, eat them, and leave without paying. He acquired so many traffic warrants that he was hounded by the state police.

Michael had always wanted to go to college. Since childhood it had been his dream to enroll at the University of Oregon in Eugene. Having completed his high school studies and received his diploma while at Fort Ord, he now wondered whether there was a chance. Ruth had moved to Eugene to be with Grandmother Ella, and in the spring of 1965 Michael decided to pay them a visit. In Eugene he was able to work for a university professor of political science, coding tests, but the pay was small, and Ruth was unable to help out. Michael's efforts to borrow money for tuition and books failed. Then when he looked at the entrance requirements for matriculation at the university, he found that his high school grades did not qualify him, and the examinations were too tough. Baffled, he returned to Portland where he wrote more bad checks—and spent a night in jail.

Michael was unemployed when he received another notice from his draft board. In those days the draft was a specter that hung over the heads of millions of young American males. He decided to skip town. His brother Kent was now married, working on an assembly line making rockets for North American Rockwell and living in Seal Beach, California, south of Los Angeles. Michael located a friend who was driving south and joined him. Michael soon fell in love with the mild climate of southern California, and he went to work delivering pizza in Long Beach. The job didn't last, so Michael, now twenty-one, began collecting unemployment compensation and bouncing from apartment to apartment, living with newly made friends.

The Beatles had just released a new song, "Nowhere Man," that captured Michael's imagination. Where was he? He was nowhere, man. He saw himself as a fun-loving, happy-go-lucky, joke-telling, woman-chasing, beer-drinking average guy. But inside he was a completely different person—lonely, empty, insecure, with no self-confidence or self-esteem, completely void of purpose or direction.

In this frame of mind Michael took a fatal step. Some

friends gave him his first hit of marijuana. Thus he was introduced to the drug culture (about which he had been warned all his life), a world that was soon to entangle him in a pit of torment.

It was a new year, 1966, and Michael came to a great decision: this was the year he would join the Beatles. Europe had never left his mind since he had watched that Ed Sullivan show. The problem was, he had no money. But he telephoned his stepfather, Ozzie, whom he had not seen for years, and asked him to help him out. "I'm having some problems," he told him. Much to Michael's surprise, Ozzie sent him a hundred dollars. With a buddy, John Summers, Michael started to hitchhike across the country. The plan was to find work on the Atlantic seaboard after which they would shoot to Europe. But they forgot one thing: nearly all of America outside of southern California was locked in winter.

They reached Illinois half frozen and headed for Aurora, where John's sister lived. Soon they found work in a machine shop in nearby Batavia, working drill presses and driving lift trucks. It was a bitter comedown for Michael. He hated it. *What am I doing here*, he mused, *living in a cheap room over a tavern, dragging out at five-thirty in the morning and walking two miles with no boots in a temperature of 24 below zero and living off thirty-five-cent cheeseburgers and fifteen-cent beers?*

As soon as he had accumulated enough money, Michael quit his job, said good-bye to John, took a bus to O'Hare airport, and caught a plane to Miami for no reason other than that he had heard it was warm in Florida. But Miami Beach was not what he had been told it was. He took a room in a Cuban refugee hotel where no one spoke English—it was all he could afford. He was also starting to grow paranoid, becoming suspicious of everyone. He would pull hairs out of his head and lay them on his suitcase to make sure no one was going through his effects. (If the hairs were moved when he returned to his room, he would know someone had been in the suitcase.) James Bond was getting to him. Thinking he could land a glamour job on a Caribbean cruise ship, he began hanging around the docks and steamship line offices, but to no avail. One ship's captain looked him over and barked, "Young man, you're not a sailor. Get out of here!"

Two weeks in Florida were enough. Michael wrote a check on a bank in Eugene, Oregon, using an account long since closed. That enabled him to fly back to Chicago. Perhaps, he thought, he could return to his job in the Batavia machine shop. On reaching Aurora he borrowed ten dollars from some girlfriends, was rehired at the shop, and survived for a week on a pound of bologna, a loaf of bread, and a gallon of milk. Then with his first paycheck he got into trouble. After spending all day Sunday drinking, he became involved in a tavern brawl and was thrown out into a snowbank in an alley. Bruised and battered, he made his way to his cheap hotel in Aurora where the woman clerk helped him to his room after he fell down the front stairs.

Two nights later Michael sat in a bar until closing time, then went out into the snow and walked to the Fox River, which divides Batavia and Aurora. He started to cross the bridge, but stepped out instead on one of the abutments and sat with his feet dangling above the dark water. Chunks of gleaming ice floated underneath him. Somehow he sensed that a crisis was approaching in his life. *Nobody knows I'm here*, he thought. *I'm drunk. My family is in splinters. There's no reason for me to live. I have no place to go except to that crummy room. I have no hope. If I were to drop into this river, who would know about it? Or care? There's no sense going on like this, drinking, fighting, messing with girls and hurting them. David talked about goals, but what goals do I have? Life is like a great big movie, and I have no part in it. I could slip over the edge and—*

Lights flashed at the end of the bridge. Michael held his breath. Perhaps he did have a part in the movie! It was a police car. They would find him. Perhaps they were even looking for him, wanting to stop him, to help him. Think of it—his attempted suicide averted at the last minute by the arrival of a rescue squad! It was like a television script. The squad car moved onto the span and drove slowly to where he was...then continued on across the bridge to the other side. Nobody saw where Michael was perched. The police were after other game—a pedestrian who had crossed the bridge ahead of them. They picked him up. Michael was disappointed, then indignant. *They don't care,* he reflected. *Nobody does, not even the cops.* But in his indignation he made up his mind not to jump. After all, he reasoned with typical MacIntosh logic, a person could freeze to death in the water with all that floating ice!

A day or so later he quit the machine shop for the last time and started west. Hitchhiking on Route 66 in midwinter was hazardous. Once he was picked up by a homosexual and made a fast exit. He was stopped by police, dropped off in the country at night with no light but the stars, befriended and fed by Texas college students, and set down by one driver at a farm crossroads where there was no traffic in any direction. Someone had told him about the lovely white sandy beaches on the west coast of Mexico, and Michael decided that whichever way a car was going, he would flag it down and eventually head for Mexico.

After spending interminable days and nights on the road, Michael arrived in Juarez, Mexico, across the Rio Grande from El Paso, Texas. In the bus depot, with his hair now quite long, he was mistaken for one of the Beatles and dubbed "El Ringo." Michael liked that. He took a bus across Mexico to Mazatlan, a west coast seaport that was fast becoming a tourist paradise. He found it as he had been told: a place with gorgeous beaches, balmy climate, and lots of young Americans on the loose.

Michael fitted easily into the surfing crowd. Someone lent him a board and he began to enjoy himself. He booked into a hotel that was overrun with outsized cockroaches and thought of moving his sleeping bag onto the beach until a friend pointed to the tracks made nightly over the sand by pythons and rats in search of garbage.

Living on tacos and Cokes, tanning his body and enjoying the surf, Michael was making the acquaintance of the "expate" California crowd when he discovered that the big topic of interest was a new drug called LSD. Michael had been reading Freud and Adler, the better to understand himself; but now a book called *Me, Myself and I* was placed in his hands. It was the account of a woman who had taken LSD under the care of a psychiatrist. Michael had never touched the drug, but he found her experiences intriguing.

One of his new friends, an attractive blonde, told him she had taken LSD several times. "I don't think I could," Michael said. "I'd go crazy or something."

"No, it's O.K.," said the surfers who were on the beach with them. "It's cool. You'd be surprised." That night he read further in *Me, Myself and I* and thought, *Maybe that drug could really help a person out, if you took it under the right conditions.*

Next day the blonde girl said, "I'm going back to California. Do you want a ride?"

"Yeah." The best times Michael had ever had were in the sun in California. *I don't ever want to be lonely again,* he thought. *I want to make something of my life, and California is the place.*

It seemed like going home. They drove in her Chevrolet Monza and arrived in Newport Beach in March 1966, a few days before Michael's twenty-second birthday. He was in a happy mood; the dark water of the Fox River was behind him.

# 7

# The Free Spirit

*California dreamin' on such a winter's day.*
The Mammas and Pappas, "California Dreamin'"

Beach bums!

No other words described them. Southern California's beaches from Santa Monica to San Diego were awash with them as they swarmed in from every state and half the free world. Like seagulls and sandpipers they stalked the golden shores and drifted with the tide. They were the environment, the two-legged part of nature. But only by a generous use of imagination could they be called a functioning part of the human race. Michael MacIntosh not only joined them, he became the paragon of beach bums. Having lost all real desire, he was the free spirit of the area.

The girl who had driven him from Mazatlan dropped Michael at Newport Beach and headed for Van Nuys and home. Since Michael had no home, he looked up a friend and found his house empty. But on the back porch, he remembered, was an outside shower; so for a long time he stood under the spray, washing off the dust of Mexico.

Michael spent that night as a guest of a former girl-friend in the women's dormitory of the new University of

California at Irvine. He set into operation a new and unique "MacIntosh housing plan"; by rotating among friends old and new, he was never without a place to sleep. As for food, when the school cafeterias closed he had other recourses—tricks he had learned at Fort Ord when he would hitchhike to Santa Cruz on weekends with other soldiers and sponge off picnickers on the beach.

"Hi, folks," he would say as he approached a couple with a bulging basket of food. "We were out swimming and someone stole our picnic basket."

"Oh, that's too bad," was the typical response. "Why don't you have some chicken and watermelon with us?"

In the daytime Michael's body became bronzed on the beaches, and his cheerful facade became more firmly fixed in place. In the evening an apartment doorbell would ring, and there he would be—friendly, blue-eyed, handsome Mike. "Hey, come on in!"

But underneath it all, the loneliness, the ache, the sense of loss hurt worse than ever.

A source of steady income materialized: Michael found he could collect pop bottles on the beach and redeem them at a local supermarket. By really working at it he could pick up three or four dollars a day, but Michael didn't work too hard. After all, rent was free, and a new chain, McDonald's, was selling hamburgers at fifteen cents each. Or he would go to a friend's house with a blue box of Kraft's macaroni and cheese and a $1.49 gallon of Red Mountain wine. He spent most of his time surfing, playing football, loafing, drinking beer and wine, telling jokes, and listening to rock music by the Rolling Stones and the Beau Brummels.

One afternoon in Newport Beach he was watching some eastern college students playing touch football on the sand next to Thirty-eighth Street and Seashore Drive. One of them said to him, "We've seen you somewhere. You're a rock-and-roll singer, aren't you?"

"Well, yeah, I used to sing with a few groups," he lied with a smile.

It was a party of eight, all college seniors or school teachers on an Easter break holiday. Michael seemed to them a humorous novelty, a real beach bum. They let him sleep in their various apartments. It seemed that all of southern California had flocked for the week either to Palm Springs or to Balboa Island, a unique beach resort on a small island in Newport Harbor. Michael's new friends invited him to go to Balboa with them. He was in an effervescent mood, laughing, partying, joking, and meeting new girls. He and his friends found an apartment near Balboa and negotiated a deal with the manager. By pulling weeds around the place, they could have it rent-free for a month. When a tiger-striped cat showed up, they adopted it and named it Fang. At the nightly parties they would introduce their "pet puma," which became something of an attraction.

The project for the month was to meet girls and more girls. In order to do so, Michael and one of his friends devised a routine. He would stand on a street corner improvising on a harmonica (which he couldn't play) and shuffling his feet in a pseudo tap dance (neither could he dance). When the girls came by, as they did by the score, Michael would engage them in silly conversation. The friend would then approach and set a football down behind one of them.

"Excuse me, I'm singing and dancing for these girls. What are you doing?" Michael would say.

"Well, pardon me, ma'am, but you dropped your football."

"It's not my football," the girl would giggle, taking the ball and being caught off-guard. The ball was passed

around, the routine worked, and they ended up knowing
each other.

"Hey, what's happening?" Michael would say. "Would
you autograph our football? Put down your name and telephone number. Would you like to go sailing?"

"Yeah."

"Do you have a boat? No? Well, would you like to go to a
party? Do you have an apartment we could use?"

If the party was to be at Michael's, sometimes six different girls they had met during the day would show up. One
would bring a gallon of wine, another the spaghetti, another the meat sauce. Extra guys would be brought in,
and everybody was happy to meet everybody else.

On one particular afternoon a girl named Laurie, a
graduate of Stephens College in Missouri, was coming
along the sidewalk. She had flown out from New York to
visit friends in Los Angeles, but when those friends threw
a marijuana party that was raided by police, Laurie (who
was not involved) chose to depart. She drove to Balboa Island, where a former Stephens classmate, Sandra Riddet,
and two girlfriends were renting a place.

From his spot on the corner, Michael noticed Laurie
coming, and saw she was cute. He tuned up his harmonica
and held out his hand. "I've got a pet puma at home," he
explained, "and it's starving. I need a little extra cash to
feed it."

"A pet puma?" Laurie was indignant. "Nobody has pet
pumas. Get away and don't bother me."

But Michael was intrigued, for she sounded like an intellectual type. He followed her down the street, playing
his harmonica and talking. He learned that she was from
the east, had graduated from Stephens, and was visiting
friends. How long was she staying? She would be return-
ing to New York in a few days. She paused in front of a
house overlooking Newport Bay, while he talked about

himself. The other girls she was visiting came out and chatted; it was all quite casual. But Michael's mind was whirring. *Eureka*, he thought, *these people have class. I've hit a gold mine!* His eye roamed over the yachts berthed in the canal that separated Balboa from the mainland, the Cape Cod houses quaintly bordering the waterfront. It seemed the high school dropout, the ex-foundry rousta-bout, the beach bum had moved into another sphere. The fairy godmother's wand had finally touched Cinderella.

"I have no money or anything," he told Laurie, "but before you go back to New York, if you want to go out on a date, give me a call. My friend can lend me his car. And if you want to pay the way, here's my number."

Two days later the telephone rang at the House of Fang. It was Laurie. "I'm only in town one more day, but tonight I'd like to go out." Michael was again introduced to the other three girls. He noticed particularly the attractive, blue-eyed, short-haired, tall blonde they called "Sandy." Michael gleaned one important fact from Laurie on the date: the following Sunday, April 16, 1966, was Sandra Rid-det's birthday, which Laurie would miss.

Michael planned his moves carefully. He looked up his collegiate friends and told them, "Let's go, you guys. There's a party Sunday at Balboa Island." And so he came, uninvited, with his friends, and Sandra didn't even re-member him. Nor did anyone else. Most of the people came from Disneyland, where Sandra had been singing in the Golden Horseshoe before she enrolled at Cal State, Long Beach.

But Michael made his mark. Using white shoe polish, he had daubed the fences and sidewalks leading to her apart-ment with the words HAPPY BIRTHDAY SANDY! He also ordered a dozen roses sent to her and charged them to her address.

During the evening Michael sat on the floor of the apartment, grinning from ear to ear, thinking, *How neat it is. How happy all these people are. They're all educated. They all have money. They're all successful.* His head swam. Around him others were laughing, smoking, drinking, and occasionally dancing. They would say to him, "What are you smiling about?" and Michael would reply, "I'm just a happy person." But to himself he admitted, *I'm miserable.*

Sandra, however, fascinated him. She was artistic, poetic, musical, and extremely intelligent. An impressive shelf of her books overlooked the room. Michael realized he was outclassed but couldn't resist the challenge. For some months he had tried to acquire a smattering of culture so he wouldn't appear so ignorant around his friends. He borrowed their class notes and their books, looked into Shakespeare and actually read Dostoevski's *Crime and Punishment.* As the evening waxed late, he sought to present to Sandra the image of an eager mind.

"I like that part in Dostoevski where he talks to the police chief and almost admits his crime."

"Oh?" said Sandra. "You like to read?"

"Oh, yeah." Michael waved his hand toward her books. "I've read most of what you have here."

At last the party ended and the guests left, but not Michael. On and on they talked, Michael and Sandra and her roommates, until everyone's story was told. It seemed that Sandra's father was president of a corporation with headquarters in Philadelphia and dealings in Europe; he had worked his way up from the laboratory to the top. Her brother was a lawyer; her mother's father had been somebody important; and Sandra herself was majoring in English, had conservative tastes, and would be touring Europe the coming summer.

Michael went home toward morning, his head in a whirl. The very leaves on the trees seemed to be growing as he looked at them. The flowers under the streetlight were changing colors. The sunrise was by far the most spectacular he had ever seen. But it was not love that gave nature its eerie aspect this Monday morning. Just before going to the party, Michael had walked across the street and bought and swallowed his first capsule of LSD. He was riding high.

Four weeks later Michael and Sandra were married, barefoot, in Las Vegas.

# 8

# Forbidden Fruit

*Eight miles high.*
The Byrds

For Sandra, Michael was forbidden fruit. All her life she had been kept away from that kind of person and lifestyle; in fact, she had hardly spent a single day that didn't have a goal or purpose to it. But Michael was different, and she found that exciting and attractive. He was the focus of her late-developing rebellion against the prim and proper lifestyle in which she had been raised, the one big act she knew would meet with her parents' disapproval.

Sandra Riddet's "plunge," as she described it, dropped her into a cold surf. No longer was the plastic bubble of family protection there to shield her. No longer could she live her cosy life doing the nice things expected of her. She had a beach bum on her hands, and the stink of marijuana was in her house.

Before life took her from one world and flung her into another, Sandra had a good thing going. Born into a conventional Methodist family in LaGrange, Illinois, she began singing in the church choir as a child and never missed a Sunday. By the time she was ready for college her father, Wilfrid Riddet, had become president of Imperial Type and Chemical Company. He shipped her off to fashionable Stephens College in Columbia, Missouri, where she majored in music, sang in school operettas and musical comedies, and thought about going on stage. She acquired an interest in art and dabbled in oil painting. Wherever she went, she took her sketch pad or easel along with her.

At the time she met Michael, Sandra had finished her two years at Stephens, worked for a time at Disneyland, and was going for a degree at Long Beach State. Like many college girls of her social and economic position, she had plans to spend the summer in Europe. When she met Michael she already had her tickets and her luggage. But it was spring break, that lovely hiatus when everything comes to a stop and fun takes over.

Michael, of course, had nothing to do, so they went walking on the beach, and he would play his guitar for her. He didn't really know how to play, but that didn't seem to matter. He made up all kinds of stories about himself, saying he was a musician in a Long Beach club or a medical student. It was a different story every day, and deep down Sandra probably knew none of them were true, but she chose to ignore or even believe them. They were just part of his charm, and she thought he was cute even though he looked exactly like what he was—a beach bum.

The fact was that Sandra hardly knew Michael at all, but in three weeks she was madly in love with him anyway. Her infatuation had begun the first time she met him; no one had ever had the same effect on her.

They started dating on April 16, and on May 13 they were married. There never was a proposal, just a suggestion—"Let's go to Las Vegas and get married"—as if it were a dare. They drove all night to Vegas, and Michael found a friend in a bowling alley, and he and another friend became the witnesses. In midmorning the four-some walked into the office of a justice of the peace to find out when they could have the ceremony. A woman seated at a desk informed them that the fee was twelve dollars, which Michael paid in pop bottle money.

Sandra had put a dress in her suitcase when she left, intending to change before the wedding. At the moment she was wearing a pair of slacks and a blouse, and Michael sported a T-shirt and jeans. Both of them were barefoot. The lady said to them, "Sit there in the hallway." In a moment a door opened at the end of the hall and a man waved them toward him. They shook hands and were invited into a small room.

"How's the weather at Balboa Island this week?" the man asked.

"Oh, it's beautiful."

Without further delay he began asking the questions and they recited the marriage vows. In five minutes it was all over, and they were married.

They had gone in just to learn the details of what they had to do to get married. Given a little more time, they probably would have decided not to get married after all. But married they now were; so they went to a tavern around the corner and had a few beers with their two witnesses, watched Art Linkletter on television, and left Las Vegas.

Before they were married, Michael had confessed to Sandra his failures, his insecurity, and his unemployed status. He tried to show her every ugly side of himself so she would know whom she was getting involved with, but her infatuation blinded her. For his part, Michael considered all her qualities and realized she was the kind of person he wanted to be with, even though he thought her to be his intellectual superior and she was definitely from a different social world. They were in love, and that plus her rebelliousness against her upbringing were all that mattered.

What fascinated Michael about Sandra was her ability to appreciate life. She helped him enjoy studying flowers, listening to the sound of waves on the beach, watching a puppy across the street or a boy throwing a ball in the air. Under her guidance, he was learning for the first time to observe closely what was going on about him. But for three days after they told each other, "I'd like to marry you," Michael sank into one of his moods of hopelessness. He had failed so many times, and he was afraid he was psychologically not strong enough to handle marriage.

The drive back to California without sleep was more a nightmare than a honeymoon. They went first to Santa Barbara, where Michael intended to look up a relative. But they pulled in exhausted and spent their wedding night in the car, Sandra sleeping in the back seat, Michael in the front. One day later they drove back to Balboa Island, where Sandra shortly took a job as waitress on a floating restaurant, the *Reuben E. Lee*, and Michael went surfing. He would go paddling by on his board and wave to her as she was carrying trays.

Their revised plan called for Sandra to make her trip to Europe in June and come back in September without telling her family what she had done. After several days of being Mrs. Michael MacIntosh, however, she was feeling so guilty and so overcome about not telling her parents that she had to call them. She was still excited by her quick marriage, but once their cover was blown, everything changed.

Two or three months of excitement followed, but actually the marriage went badly from the beginning. Sandra had deceived herself into thinking that she was the key who was going to turn Michael the right way. She was sympathetic toward his unhappy childhood, and she also saw he had a great deal of potential, charm, and ability. It soon became clear, however, that not only was she not the one to change him, but that he had no desire to change.

# 9

# Completely Gone

*Reform only yourself.*
Montaigne

In the comic strip "Bringing Up Father," which is now venerated as early Americana, Maggie married Jiggs to reform him. It didn't work. It never does. Sandra MacIntosh could love Michael passionately, but she could not move him. After the ceremony he continued to be a sandpiper, wandering on the beach. He was of course totally unprepared for the shocks that followed marriage. Daily deliveries flooded the little post office on Balboa Island, and the rented cottage began to burgeon with silver trays, candelabra, and all manner of expensive wedding gifts from the east. Boxes were shipped in direct from Philco and Corningware. And the more that came in, the more the thought of eventually meeting Sandra's father intimidated Michael.

But the young man's shocks were nothing to the reaction of the senior Riddets. They were under the impression that their only daughter was already involved with someone else. The more they found out about the bizarre episode in Las Vegas, the harder time they had believing it. But as conscientious and loving parents they determined to make the best of it, and in a short time they arrived in California, loaded with more gifts for the bride and bridegroom. After all, they reasoned, Sandra was their daughter, and she had a good head on her shoulders. She must have known what she was doing.

Wilfrid Riddet discerned right away that Michael was a strange young man and something was wrong. Michael lied and told him he was a stable person and was planning to return to the University of Oregon, but Riddet saw through it all. After a couple of months Sandra quit her job and they drove a secondhand Volkswagen bus back to Philadelphia for a visit. As soon as Michael got a look at the Riddets' impressive home with its white pillars and virgin forest behind, his heart sank. He knew there was no way he could relate to these people. The house had a little apartment in the basement; and one day when Sandra (at her husband's urging) was out job-hunting and he was just hanging around, Mrs. Riddet came downstairs and blew up at him.

"What's the matter with you, Mike?" she demanded. "Why aren't you out working? How do you expect to support our daughter? What do you intend to do?"

Michael told her he guessed he would have a talk with her husband. Anything to get her off his back! That night he and Mr. Riddet sat down together in the beautifully furnished living room.

"What do you want to do with your life, Mike?" his father-in-law inquired in a kindly tone.

Michael had to think of something. "I've always wanted to be an airline pilot," he said finally.

"Well! There's an airfield right near here. Why don't you sign up for flying lessons?"

Michael did apply at the local field and took lessons. Eventually he even made his first solo flight. But meanwhile he and Sandra both got jobs at a Jewish summer day camp. Weeks passed, and it became clear to all parties that things weren't working out too well. The newlyweds needed to be on their own. So Michael and Sandra drove the bus back to the West Coast, found a little apartment above a garage in Newport Beach, acquired two kittens and three dogs, and tried again.

This time Michael found a job. He applied at a steel foundry and talked to the owner's daughter who, after sizing him up, told him, "I think you're a little too sharp to be working in a foundry. We're looking for a young man to train as our buyer. Would you be interested?"

"Well, I guess so," said Michael. But office work turned out to be a bore. They assigned him to different departments and he caught on quickly—usually too quickly. In the accounting department he found a sixty-eight-thousand-dollar error the first day and brought it to a superior's attention. It was covered up. In inventory control he suggested ways to improve the record-keeping, which were not appreciated. He asked for a raise and it was refused, so he quit.

The next job was with an electronics firm in Anaheim. Michael was to be an expediter. The Vietnam War was on, and the United States government was the chief customer. Michael soon discovered that some orders had been placed six months earlier and had not been filled. As an expediter, he did what was expected of him. He called people and told them, "Hey, you're not getting the stuff out. What's wrong? Let's move it!"

As a result, one of his bosses got very upset with him. Michael didn't understand why at first, but then he concluded that the people there were underworked and were trying to hang onto their jobs. The man told Michael, "We need more time, more money, and more people." And he warned him not to bother the other employees any more. Michael tried to be helpful and fit in, but once again he found himself upsetting the status quo. Rivalries developed, and he chose to depart.

Next Michael answered a newspaper advertisement for a car salesman, and this time he found himself in his element. In his first week he sold five cars and seemed to have tapped a natural talent. He had never sold cars before, but he possessed a gift of gab and seemed to tell the right stories. He would inform the customers, "It's cute, it fits your personality, you need it for your image, and it's only two hundred more than the other one." If it was a used car, he could come up with excellent reasons why it didn't run right. But he soon decided the dealer was taking advantage of him and not paying him what he should, so Michael switched jobs and started working at another car lot.

Here he did better; in his first year he won an award from Fiat for being a top salesman. His name was painted on the window of the agency, and he was presented with a pin that had a ruby in it. They also gave him the best demonstrator car to drive; but he got more enjoyment out of a motorcycle he had picked up. His shaggy dog, Arnold, a cross between a golden retriever and a standard poodle, would sit on the gas tank and put his paws on the handlebars; and they would go tooling through the neighborhood.

Obviously Michael was not ready to join the establishment. He had used no LSD during his visit to Philadelphia, but he had been reading Timothy Leary on controlled psychedelic experience, and when they returned to the coast he resumed his experimenting. The Riddets, happy that their son-in-law was working at last, purchased a lovely new three-bedroom home for them in Irvine's exclusive University Park, but it only heightened the tension. *Everything is being given to me*, Michael thought bitterly. *I don't have to earn a thing.* He went back to Timothy Leary and found that his book was actually a Western version of the Tibetan Book of the Dead, which was intended to prepare people for death. He listened to the new Beatles album, "Revolver," and when John Lennon sang about turning off one's mind, relaxing, and floating down the stream, Michael recognized that the words were taken from Leary's book. He now had a link between the Beatles and LSD and began taking the drug once a week.

After he became a car salesman, he discovered that all the other salesmen drank, and he began to join them. Soon he was into his old drinking habits. Sandra had quickly become aware that her husband was involved in drugs, and when they moved into the new home she noticed a change for the worse.

It became extremely difficult for Sandra to carry on a serious discussion with Michael. If they had any disagreement, he would become defensive and leave the house. Two or three days later he would come back, usually at 2:30 or 3:00 in the morning, after the bars had closed. Drugs like LSD were still fairly new at that time, and Sandra didn't realize how dangerous they were.

In addition to liquor and hallucinatory drugs, he had now begun to dabble in TM (transcendental meditation), which was appealing to thousands of Americans. Its widespread following was due almost entirely to one guru, the Maharishi Mahesh Yogi, who was founding hundreds of meditation centers in dozens of countries. The Maharishi was proving highly attractive, especially to young people. He seemed almost like a messiah, and Michael felt a need to have contact with something spiritual. These were the sixties, and the whole country was trying new things. Michael managed to get Sandra interested in it, mainly because it didn't have anything to do with drugs. They went to the training sessions and read the autobiography of Paramahansa Yogananda, the founder of the Self-Realization Fellowship. But Sandra's interest in it was short-lived, and she soon concluded it was a hoax. So they disagreed over that, too, and Michael took off again.

In spite of all the turmoil caused by Michael's habits and lifestyle, there are some tender memories of those days that both cherish. They were so young and full of life. The separations would be followed by tearful and loving reunions. Then God blessed them with a child, and a new and marvelous bond was established between them. By the time little Melinda was born (August 28, 1967), they had moved into the charming stucco house the Riddets had bought them, a kind and quality of house Michael had never lived in since he was born.

A year or so later during one of their reunions (which were becoming less frequent), Sandra became pregnant again. This discovery made her determined to see if she could salvage their marriage. Divorce was totally opposed to her view of life, and she hoped that with an all-out effort on her part some way could be found to work things out. She telephoned Michael in Laguna Beach, where he was staying with friends, and asked him to come over. She tried to have a sensible conversation with him, but there was no dealing with him. She finally said to him, "Here I am carrying your child and taking care of your home. Don't you love me at all?"

He looked at her with glazed eyes and said, "I just love everybody."

Sandra couldn't handle it. She put her furniture in storage, rented the house, and left in four days for Philadelphia, taking Mindi with her. But before leaving for the airport, she took a teary, hysterical telephone call from Michael. "Please, this is the biggest mistake of my life. I can't live without you!" But Sandra looked at her little girl and her own swelling body and thought, *I just can't go through it again.*

Once settled in Philadelphia, and resuming the even tenor of family life she had always known, Sandra began to realize how odd and erratic the whole adventure had been. Obviously the marriage was a shocking mistake, an aberration doomed to disaster. To confirm her judgment, Michael wrote her a rambling letter saying he had just met the Beatles. He added a little note to his daughter Mindi, telling her that he and John Lennon had just written her a lullaby.

When David James MacIntosh made his appearance on February 28, 1969, in Philadelphia, the Riddets promptly telephoned their lawyer son in Santa Ana, California, with the news. By coincidence on that same day Michael walked into his brother-in-law's office carrying a briefcase.

Jim Riddet greeted him with, "Today you're a father, you know, Mike. Sandy had a baby. You have a son named David."

"Wow," said Michael vacantly. "Thank you." He then proceeded to unravel his latest hallucinatory fantasy. He had been out on the desert, he said, working with the CIA on some flying saucers that had been sighted there. He had brought Riddet a lot of important documents so that if anything happened to him, Jim was to contact the CIA or the FBI and they would have a pension plan for Sandy and take care of her!

Riddet was flabbergasted. "What are you talking about?" he demanded. With that Michael opened his briefcase on the desk and dumped out a lot of papers. They included an old insurance policy, a dog license, a validated parking ticket, an expired passport, and some other papers of equal value.

"This will take care of it," said Michael. "I'll be going now."

But Jim Riddet wouldn't let him go. He took him to dinner and talked to him at some length. That night Jim called his parents in Philadelphia and told them, "Mike's gone. He's just completely gone!"

# 10

# The Police Station

*We all live in a yellow submarine.*
The Beatles, "Yellow Submarine"

Before Sandra and Mindi left for Philadelphia, a disturbing incident brought the old element of terror back into Michael's life. During his salad days he had dated a young woman whose boyfriend was serving a prison term in San Quentin. It was one of many mistakes he had made, and with the passing of time he forgot about it. But now the man had been released, and he was on the warpath. Michael was at the car lot one evening when he received a call from the police, telling him that someone had broken into his house.

He arrived home to find that Sandra and Mindi were safe, but a crowd had gathered and police and sheriff's cars were on the scene. Investigators were taking fingerprints and photographers were taking pictures. A man had come with a tire iron, looking for Michael, and had broken in the front door. Neighbors were aroused, and as a result the intruder had driven off with his girlfriend, but not until his license number had been noted.

Michael was sure the man was the ex-convict, so he went outside and told the police, "Let's just forget it. I made some mistakes and my mistakes have caught up with me." Afterward he decided he had better try to smooth things over, so he looked up his adversary and found his telephone number. "I know you're mad," Michael told him, "and you're after me, and I'm sorry. I'm sure God wouldn't have anybody kill anybody. I've talked to the police, and why don't we just forget the whole thing?"

The man's response was a threat. "You'd just better hope the police get to me before I get to you!"

Next day the sheriff sent an investigator to see Michael at the car lot. "I've talked to this guy," Michael said, "and he's still threatening to kill me."

"If I were you," said the investigator, "I'd keep away from him. He has bad friends, and he's a tough character."

"Aren't you going to do anything?" Michael asked.

"Just keep away from him."

Shortly afterward Sandra and Mindi left for Philadelphia, and Michael had to move out of the Irvine house. He was selling well and making several hundred dollars a week, but one day, after he had taken some LSD, he told his boss about the impending divorce and asked if he could get away.

"Sure," he was told, "just get in a corner and don't listen to anybody's advice. Take a few days and get your head together." Michael took that advice, rented a place down by the beach, and with his bag of LSD he sat and watched the waves.

One day a man he recognized came up to him and said, "MacIntosh, what are you doing alive?"

"What do you mean?"

"Your friend has put a contract out on you."

"You're kidding."

"I'm not kidding. He was at our place when the FBI

raided it and arrested him for smuggling dope. He had just got through telling two Mexican guys to get you."

Michael's heart sank. He became suspicious of people. He wondered how it would happen—would they shoot him, stab him, or break his arms and throw him over a cliff? It affected his job; he couldn't sell cars anymore. His roach-ridden little beach house became his hideaway. He increased his drug intake and made it a daily dosage. Thinking he would "try to find" himself, he started attending the popular rock-and-roll concerts, but it was a whirlpool that kept getting deeper.

One night he drove to the Shrine auditorium in Los Angeles and found the place packed with kids listening to four different rock groups. The strobe lights were flashing and giant screens were showing rapid-fire stills of flowers, Hitler, soldiers parachuting, and other scenes, most of them ugly.

*There is something bigger than a concert going on here,* Michael thought. *These people are putting hate into the audience without the audience knowing it.*

He climbed up on one of the stages where the Vanilla Fudge group was playing. The pills made him bold, and he knew the musicians were equally loaded; but behind the giant screen he found something that truly amazed him. A wholly different group from those dancing out front were squatting on the floor looking at the backside of the screen. They seemed quite at home, and they were watching pictures of Satan, with goatee, pitchfork, and grotesque demons all around. Kneeling on the platform, Michael prayed, "God, if you're real, please get me out of this. There is a conspiracy going on. I need a Christian girl to help me, one I can explain this to. This concert is nothing but a front to brainwash people and sell drugs."

The concert ended and people started to leave. Michael,

well spaced out, went up to a man and asked him where he could find a Christian girl. The man said, "Go stand in that line there."

After he had stood in line a while another man came and asked him, "What's your number?"

"What are you talking about?"

"Your stage or union number."

It turned out they were handing out paychecks to the people in line. Michael studied them and recalled seeing them in the auditorium. They were all dressed like hippies, wearing freak haircuts and coveralls; the girls wore T-shirts and no bras. They were actually actors, serving as trend-setters to impress the patrons and teach them what they should be like. Once the truth struck him, Michael began yelling, "You're all phonies!" A man quickly stepped up and warned him, saying he was a narcotics officer and if Michael didn't leave, he would take him downtown. He left.

That evening, a friend introduced him to Ron, the long-haired leader of the mystic cult that soon afterward took Michael to the desert to wait for flying saucers to land at Giant Rock Airport. Ron and his followers were talking up heroin, but Michael wasn't interested. He had known a pusher in Huntington Beach who sprinkled heroin into his marijuana to hook teen-age girls. Then the girls would come back with, "Hey, I need some more of that other kind; I'm not getting high." But Ron's people were also into yoga and Zen, and Michael wanted to hear more about that.

Three weeks after his trip to Yucca Valley, Michael's friend Rick, who drove the Volkswagen van, gave him some pills and dropped him off at Ron's house. It was then that Michael had the nightmarish experience of feeling the side of his head blown off by a gun blast—a feeling that persisted for two years and convinced him for much of that time that he was dead. Rick came back for Michael late in the evening and dropped him off at his house in Huntington Beach. He woke up his brother Kent. "Help me, please."

"What's the matter?"

"I've been shot in the head."

"You *what*?" Kent turned on the light and said, "You're O.K. Don't tell me you've been taking that LSD garbage again."

"I have, but it's real. Please just love me and help me."

Kent was kind and gentle with his younger brother and talked with him when he couldn't sleep. Michael would wake up in the night hearing the gun go off all over again and start to panic. He would get up and walk out into the front yard and look at the stars and slap himself, just to make sure it was his body he was inhabiting.

After a few days Michael moved to Laguna Beach at the invitation of some friends. While he was there he listened to a new Beatles record, and the old conviction came back in all its fantasy:

*I belong with the Beatles!* He was on his usual high, and to prove his point he decided to do something different. Going to a well-known "head shop" in Laguna Beach called "Mystic Arts," he walked into the meditation room. There he thought he heard voices telling him to go down to the beach and baptize himself in the ocean. He did so. Next the spirit voices told him that the Beatles were in town and were located somewhere in a Laguna Beach hotel. Michael began a wild search for them, but it proved fruitless. At last he returned to the house where he was staying, collected all the rock-and-roll records he had with him, and walked out and stood on the Pacific Coast highway, handing them out to the hippies he met. He even wandered out into the bumper-to-bumper traffic, giving the peace sign.

Late that afternoon Michael reached the end of the trail. He walked into the Laguna Beach police station and spoke to the receptionist. "Ma'am," he said, "I'm with the Beatles, and they're in town doing a nude pop art reproduction of the resurrection of Jesus Christ in a yellow submarine."

She said, "What?"

Michael said, "Well, you're going to get phone calls because I just walked nude up Coast highway, and that was my part for the Beatles."

She asked, "Would you mind just telling that to the sergeant?"

He did, and the sergeant of police said, "Would you tell that to the lieutenant?" It was just like the movies.

Michael spoke to the lieutenant, who had been warned, and his reply was, "Well, we'd like to take you to see some friends. Would you mind going with us?"

"No," said Michael, "but when Paul, John, George, and Ringo get here, would you tell them where I am?"

"Oh, sure," said the lieutenant. Michael was then driven to the Orange County Medical Center.

# 11

# Momentous Discovery

*I'm goin' through changes—changes in my mind.*
Chuck Girard, "Changes"

At Orange County Medical Center Michael was put on hold for seventy-two hours, during which he was supposed to be kept under observation. It was evening when he arrived, and he was placed in a tank with a number of other patients behind a locked door. Not wishing to fall asleep in such bizarre surroundings, he began exercising with push-ups and jumping jacks until two orderlies in white coats arrived with large red pills.

"Don't!" pleaded Michael. "I'll do anything. Just don't sedate me."

"O.K., then quit the jumping and exercising."

Soon they returned with some juice, which was also medicated. He refused it. They then shifted him to a room that contained a bed with straps on it. Again Michael pleaded: "Please, whatever you do, don't strap me down. I'll be quiet. I won't do anything."

There was no sleep for him that night.

The next day the other patients talked to him so strangely that Michael was convinced the mental ward was filled with demons and evil spirits. He was escorted to an evaluating psychiatrist and then to a full board of psychiatrists and was asked questions. He repeated his tale of joining the Beatles and being shot in the head. The consensus was that Michael should be admitted for his own good, and he was given a paper to sign. He wept again, because after four years of taking drugs he knew he was at the end of his rope.

He signed.

The conclusion of the evaluation board was that Michael should be diagnosed a paranoid schizophrenic. He spent a week at the medical center, undergoing tests and hypnosis, after which he was released to outpatient status. For the next ten months he was assigned to a Newport Beach psychologist and paid weekly visits. The hypnotic probing of childhood experiences proved helpful; it explained behavioral trends and fear reactions that had often puzzled him. Memories long buried were recalled to the threshold of consciousness. The "shot in the head" was traced to a possible desire for self-destruction.

Michael balked at the prescribed treatment at a major point: he refused all medication after one dosage, claiming the medicine made him crazier than drugs ever had. And with drugs he was finished forever; the hoped-for "good trip" that would take him "into the light" had turned into a bummer that threw him. Acid flashes did continue to recur and caused him to fade in and out of reality. Sometimes when he was shaving his image would seem to disappear off the mirror. Migraine headaches were a daily occurrence. Many, many times he would relive the horror of feeling the side of his head blown off.

With his family gone and the Irvine house sold by the Riddets, Michael went back to the house in Huntington Beach, which he shared with his brother Kent and several of his friends. He obtained another job selling cars but it did not last long—his attitude was a little too crazy for the owner. So instead of earning a thousand dollars a week, he began collecting unemployment compensation and living on food stamps. He hocked his guitar. At night he would drive around the back streets of Orange County cities, drinking six-packs of beer and trying to convince himself that his head wasn't blown off. The next morning's hangover, painful as it was, somehow felt reassuring: he was still alive.

When the ten months of treatment were up, the psychologist informed Michael that he had progressed sufficiently to be assigned to group therapy. His speech was less halting and his body, finally rid of unhealthy chemicals, gave some promise of recovering from the abuse to which it had been subjected. Michael reported regularly to the sessions where he engaged in dialogue with other patients, some of whom were struggling with problems of identity or insecurity, while others were attempting to rescue their marriages. Each week during this period Michael managed to scrape up twenty-five dollars for the psychologist's fee. After seven months he decided he should discontinue all treatment.

Michael's thoughts after seventeen months of therapy were, "O.K., I had a bad trip. The acid has left me mentally crippled for life, but I've got to accept the facts and live with them even if it means pain and agony."

During his hospital stay the doctors had asked Michael, "Do you have a plan for the future?" and he had replied, "I would like to be a songwriter." Even though his world had collapsed, he still enjoyed music. Perhaps he could work up sound tracks that would set the mood for different events. He might even break into the motion picture industry. The more he thought about music, the more he liked the idea. Sandra had taught him to enjoy beauty in nature; now he wanted to follow that path. He would become an aesthete, a lover of poetry and music.

Kent had enrolled in Orange Coast Junior College, a recently established small college sandwiched between I-405 and the Pacific Ocean. Kent was becoming involved in a radical movement known as the Students for a Democratic Society. Michael had no interest in such activity, but he visited the campus with his brother and decided he might try to learn something about music. He applied and was accepted as a student, and for the next four-and-a-half months he made his only contact with higher education. The five courses he selected were psychology, philosophy, music, speech, and cinema. He managed to maintain a B average, only to drop out after completing the spring semester. But before he closed the door on his formal education and left the campus, Michael made a momentous discovery.

He met some Christians.

It didn't make sense to him. He would see these people in his classes, carrying their Bibles and talking about the Lord. Bibles on campus? He had never run into such people. Because he was still somewhat paranoid, he became suspicious of them. Perhaps they were Communists using reverse psychology to make a mockery of religion. Perhaps their Bibles were hollow and they were dealing in drugs. It never occurred to Michael that a young person would carry a Bible to college. It seemed so foreign! And their looks troubled him, for they had long hair and looked like hippies; but he had to admit they were happy people and full of love. In all his involvement in the drug culture at the rock concerts and elsewhere, he had never seen the peace and happiness that these men and women seemed to have. And when he talked to them about it, they credited it all to Jesus Christ.

One young man particularly impressed him. He said his name was Henry Cutrona, and he looked like Paul Mc-Cartney. He was thin, with dark hair and brown eyes, and he was the happiest person Michael had ever met. The man just bubbled over with the Lord. He was light-spirited, jovial, an excellent guitar player, and a good singer. Just a free spirit! Henry wrote his own songs and would sing them sitting on the planters outside the school cafeteria. He was very uninhibited in his witness for Jesus, and Michael was intrigued by him.

For the first time Michael was hearing songs about Jesus written in the contemporary rock style of Buffalo Springfield, Moody Blues, and Crosby, Stills, and Nash—groups that had become part of his life. The effect was magnetic. He began attending concerts of singing groups that visited the campus, including Love Song and Andrae Crouch and the Disciples. Singer Chuck Girard's testimony particularly impressed him. Michael was not a Christian; he had a long way to go; he was neither reading his Bible nor attending church. But he had a new love, and music became its expression. He would compose simple tunes, put words to them, and play them on the guitar or the piano in his music class.

One day shortly after the tragic Kent State campus confrontation of 1970, a political rally was held at Orange Coast Junior College to protest President Nixon's policies and American participation in the Vietnam War. Various off-campus speakers were introduced from neighboring state universities. As sentiment began to build, hundreds of students and faculty gathered in the free-speech area. A small group ran to the flagpole, intending to lower the flag. Seeing the majority of students standing dumbfounded, Michael became excited and sought out the dean of students.

"Hey," he said, "everyone else under the sun is speaking. Can I say something?" Permission granted, he climbed on stage, took the microphone, and faced the audience.

"Do you know what you people look like?" he asked.

"No, what do we look like?" they shouted back.

"You look like a bunch of sheep without a shepherd!"

The crowd was startled. Most of them (and that included Michael) did not know he was quoting Scripture. "These people know what they're doing here. You don't. You're following them!" He named some of the leaders of the antiwar movement present. The crowd began to murmur.

In a flash it occurred to Michael that if he could inject the name of Jesus Christ in the situation, the atmosphere would be changed and the rally somehow defused. "Since so many others have spoken today," he shouted, "the next thing I expect to hear is that Jesus Christ is walking down Harbor Boulevard, and He's going to come up here and talk!"

What the students of Orange Coast Junior College thought of this strange speech may never be known, but the crowd's mood did seem to alter and some students began drifting away. The threat to the flag faded. Afterward some of the long-haired Christian students came to Michael and asked him, "Are you a Christian?"

"Of course! I'm an American." At that point in time, being a Christian and an American seemed to him equivalent if not identical.

"Are you born again?"

The confusion that drugs had created in Michael's mind kept him from understanding the implication of the question, and his dabblings in Eastern religious philosophy only added to his bewilderment. "Do you mean reincarnated?" he asked. "Not really."

"Oh. That's all we wanted to know." The long-haired ones left with their Bibles; but from that day Michael was marked, and he found himself making new friends. He liked them. He decided not to be embarrassed to be seen in their company (a major step) even though Jesus seemed to be all they talked about. He would listen to their music and hear what they had to say.

One of the things they said was, "Would you like to go to Calvary Chapel?"

# 12

# That's My Daddy!

*I'm picking up the pieces once again.*
Eric Nelson, "Picking up the Pieces"

After the birth of her son, Sandra MacIntosh realized she had to get her life together. She had a family to support for the next twenty years. The first step was obvious: she had to shake the bootless and unserviceable Michael Kirk MacIntosh out of her life. A California divorce was set in motion by her attorney brother, Jim Riddet. The court issue once settled, she faced another decision. Since her roots were in Illinois and she had never lived in the east, Philadelphia held nothing for her. She was still on the books as a student at Long Beach State in California. So, accompanied by her babies and her ever-loving parents, she boarded a plane to establish her home in California. Her parents helped her settle in an apartment in Tustin, south of Los Angeles, after which they flew back to Pennsylvania and began sending her checks. Sandra hired a woman to come in during the day and resumed her studies at Long Beach State.

The day before she gave birth to David, Sandra had received a quite rational, but devastating, letter from Michael. He told her that the district court had ordered him to pay child support, and he was not paying it, that he didn't like the idea and wanted no ties of any kind, that he would relinquish all legal rights to the children and didn't really care if he ever saw them again. He felt Sandra's parents could provide for them better than he ever could.

The letter was especially heartbreaking for Sandra, because she knew he loved Mindi, yet felt he just had to get out. She also knew what he would lose, and what the children would lose. *He doesn't deserve the children*, she thought, *but I want so much for him to love them and for them to be a part of him. Crazy as he is, he is their dad, and that's better than nothing at all.*

At the moment, however, she was not up to facing him. She had school on her mind and wanted to start building her future. What she did not know was that her ex-husband was in touch with her brother, Jim Riddet. So the first time the telephone rang in the Tustin apartment, it was Michael on the line.

When she heard his voice, she felt a combination of excitement and fear. She didn't want him to come over, but she did want him to find her. She wanted to show him his son, yet she was afraid of having a relationship with him. She even worried about having the children around him. But hearing his voice sent her heart down to her feet. She told him he had a son, which he already knew, and then she didn't know what else to say.

Michael showed up outside the screen door and Mindi spotted him. "That's my daddy!" There were hugs for the little girl but no kissing between parents. They sat and stared at each other. Sandra saw the torment in his eyes, and it cut her to the heart. *He's not well*, she thought. *He's done it all, tried everything, and there's nothing left. He can't talk. He's not coherent. His sentences—he can't finish them. He's a truly broken spirit. The cocky kid who went his own way and blew his mind on drugs is no more.*

*And I'm more afraid of him than ever.*

It was an awkward scene, yet at the same time Sandra found it exciting. Even when he was so messed up, Michael still fascinated her. There was always a little spark. As for Mindi, her father had not seen her since she was a year old, and the instant rapport and affection between them deeply moved Sandra. She watched Michael pick up his eight-week-old son and hug him, and saw the tears form in his eyes. She listened to the pitiful, childlike quality of his speech as he tried to get something across to her. Then suddenly he departed, leaving Sandra in emotional confusion.

Sandra went back to college and started rebuilding her life. For the next several months Michael would show up sporadically. She never knew when he would appear. Once in a while they would look at each other and feel a tug, and romantic thoughts would grip them, but nothing developed. For Sandra there were no future plans involving Michael. He was just out of the hospital and trying to get well, and she was busy at school. The lifestyle he had chosen had destroyed his mind and, she felt, their relationship along with it.

# 13

# Star Back into Orbit

*Little pilgrim...you found your way back home.*
Love Song, "Little Pilgrim"

As a teen-ager Michael had sometimes liked to wander in the famous Roman Catholic wooded retreat in the heart of Portland called "The Sanctuary of Our Sorrowful Mother," but better known as "the Grotto." Usually accompanied by a girlfriend named Patricia, he would drop in after school and visit the stations of the cross, then slip into the chapel and say a prayer. He did so frequently following the death of his brother David. It was one of the tender interludes in a tormented adolescence. The officiating priest was friendly and dubbed the pair "Saint Mike and Saint Pat."

Prayer had always come easily to Michael, although he could never be sure God was listening. At difficult times, such as when he was staring at a picture of his dead brother or retching from a ghastly drug trip or reading a heartbreaking letter from an ex-girlfriend, it seemed to him his prayers were bouncing off a sky of brass. Still, he liked the feeling that prayer gave him; and on his twenty-sixth birthday, March 26, 1970, he thought he would like once again to find a quiet church and say a prayer. A year had passed since Sandra and the children had returned to California. He had just received a bittersweet birthday telephone call from Sandra the night before. She said she had baked a cake, and would he like to come over to Tustin and enjoy it—and see the children?

He would.

At the time Michael was still living in Huntington Beach and had picked up a road-weary 1948 Buick station wagon known as a surf wagon or "woody." It was quite a comedown from the sports cars he used to sell so successfully. Riding with him on his weekend pleasure jaunts to the beaches, and just about everywhere else, was his comical poodle-retriever, Arnold. Michael set out that afternoon with his scruffy companion alongside and stopped first to look up a blonde girlfriend in Newport Beach. He found her sitting in her sports car with her brother, smoking a joint.

"Take a hit, Mike," she said.

"No. I don't want to smoke dope any more."

"Why not?"

"I don't need it. I've got Jesus."

What Michael really meant was that he was off drugs, and this was a cool way of putting it. He drove on to Costa Mesa and pulled into the parking lot of Calvary Chapel. He was curious about the church because he had heard a lot about it. The building was located in a field of string beans on the border of Costa Mesa and Santa Ana. The parking lot was empty. Leaving Arnold in the woody, Michael walked across the Spanish-style courtyard to the front entrance. The sanctuary was empty except for a cleaning woman. At the front of the church he boldly mounted three steps to the platform and knelt at the communion table. An open Bible and a menorah rested upon it. Michael read a psalm from the Bible, then prayed silently. After a few moments he returned to his car enveloped once again in the quiet peace he had known years before in the Grotto. He had turned down a joint and had used the name of Jesus. It felt good.

Climbing into the his trusty woody, Michael started it up but discovered it would not move. The emergency brake was apparently frozen. He got out, lifted the hood and tinkered, then crawled under the car and attacked the brake rod with a wrench. Nothing happened. By the time he emerged from underneath, serenity had evaporated and prayers were forgotten. He filled the air with hearty curses and gave the woody a swift kick. This set Arnold to barking furiously. The dog leaped from the car and Michael was forced to chase him and toss him back in. When the contrary brake finally broke loose, Michael was grimy and disgusted. He proceeded toward Tustin in a chastened mood. The best the birthday party could do, he sensed, was to show him what he had lost. And so it proved. The children ran to greet him and he played with them, wrestled on the floor with them, kissed them, laughed with them, and all the while sadness constricted his heart. Little conversation passed between Sandra and Michael. He stayed for dinner, blew out the candle on his cake, and that was it.

Three weeks passed, and one day Henry Cutrona spoke to Michael in music class. "Hey, Love Song is on tonight at Calvary Chapel."

"Yeah?" A long pause. Michael had heard the group sing and play and knew all about them; they had achieved wide popularity in southern California. "I wouldn't mind hearing them again."

By this time the woody was temporarily immobilized, and Michael was reduced to a bicycle. He stood up a date for the evening and pedaled his way ten miles from Huntington Beach to Calvary Chapel, but was hardly prepared for what awaited his arrival. The church sanctuary, designed for 350 persons, was jammed with over a thousand; and what was most amazing, they were all young and casually dressed. Further, they were singing their hearts out and lifting their hands in the air.

*Something's wrong here,* he thought. *Church people don't look like this. Where are the white shirts, the conservative suits, the bow ties, and wing-tip shoes? Where are the girls with white gloves and ribbons in their hair? Where are the old people? The robed preacher—where is he? And the choir? How come no hymnbooks? This place is wholesome. That's it, wholesome. The people are young and alive and happy. Not square. They're not embarrassed to be here, not embarrassed about Jesus.*

Love Song finished their concert, were enthusiastically applauded, and left the stage with their instruments. Their place was taken by a long-haired, bearded man wearing a hippie-style shirt and jeans and carrying a Bible. He couldn't have been more than twenty-one years old. This was Lonnie Frisbie, a hippie who had come to Christ in the Haight-Ashbury district of San Francisco and was later befriended by Pastor Chuck Smith. Chuck used the young man's gift of communicating to reach the flower-power generation with the gospel. To Michael the man looked like the paintings of Jesus he had seen, and he conveyed a kind of authority that Michael didn't seem to mind.

As the message began, Michael looked around. People seemed to be absorbed in listening. Bibles were open. He studied some of the faces, almost all serious, but some smiling as if they knew a secret. The atmosphere was electric. What was going on? To Michael the speaker's message was no different from what he had heard as a boy in the Montavilla Baptist Church. Same old gospel; nothing had changed that he could tell. The language was more up-to-date, and there was no doubt that the man could deliver the message. But at the end there was the same old invitation, just as Michael remembered it: "Does anybody here want to receive Jesus Christ as your Savior and Lord? I want you to stand right now."

Fifty or more people stood immediately, and Michael twitched. He was seated on the floor, his back in a corner, and was virtually hidden from the front. It was the only spot he could find. *I'm not going to join them,* he thought to himself. *I know all this. I did it once before back in Portland; and anyway, there's no room. I couldn't stand if I wanted to. It's just too humiliating. I'm not a teen-ager; I'm twenty-six years old. If I stand up with these people, I know what it means. What girl would want to date me if she knew I was a Christian? Why should I do it? No way am I going to stand up!*

Now the speaker was looking over the congregation, and his hand was moving back and forth. "Is there anybody here tonight," he asked, "who has left God? Maybe as a young boy or girl you knew Him, and now you've left Him. Would you want to know Him tonight personally?" Those words landed in the target area. Michael remembered waiting for the angels to come through the Oregon clouds, and the teacher who wept because he, Michael, had eternal life. His heart was struck and pierced. "God," he whispered, "that's You. Only You knew that. And You knew I was thinking about it."

Something was indeed happening in the universe. It happens every time a human being finds his way home. A wandering star was coming back into orbit. The freaked-out flower child, the apotheosis of the lost generation, was about to turn into a servant of the Most High. Whatever his reservations, Michael knew his moment of decision had come. There on the floor in the remotest corner of the packed church, Michael MacIntosh surrendered his life to Jesus Christ, not as a boy, but as a man. This time the war was over. He had put down his gun; the capitulation was complete. He was forever changed.

# 14

# All You Need Is Love

*...the love of God has been poured out in our hearts by*
*the Holy Spirit who was given to us.*
Romans 5:5

Lonnie Frisbie told those who were standing to leave by
the side entrance and go to another building in the courtyard where he would pray with them. More than one hundred people responded and walked out of the sanctuary.
Michael was one of them. He soon found himself wedged
into a small Sunday school room crowded with people.
Since there was no room to sit, they stood quietly, somewhat like tourists in a Disneyland mystery house, wondering what would happen next.

Michael was uncomfortable. Most of those in the room
were a few years younger than himself. He wondered
what he looked like to them—a shipwrecked sailor, an
emotional derelict, perhaps? Certainly a failure. But a
quick glance around disclosed that no one was paying the
slightest attention to him. Lonnie had walked up to the
blackboard and was holding a piece of chalk. "Tonight,"
he said soberly, "you have given your hearts to God. You
believe in His Son, Jesus Christ. That means, according to

the Scriptures, you are saved; you are God's children." He recited several texts underscoring the truth of their salvation, including John 1:12: "As many as received Him, to them He gave the right to become children of God...."

Michael began to feel a little better.

The speaker drew on the blackboard an upside-down waterglass. "I want to tell you," he said, "about the fullness of the power of God's Spirit that He has available for you tonight."

Michael didn't know what he was talking about.

Two more glasses were drawn, one shown lying on its side, one upright. "Your life," he went on, "is like a glass. If it's turned upside down like this, no water can get in; it just splashes off the base. If the glass is turned sideways like this, it still can't get in. But," (pointing to the third glass) "if it's straight up like this, open at the top, then the water can come in and fill it. And that's what the Holy Spirit wants to do. He wants to pour out God's love and fill you to overflowing."

As he continued to talk about the Holy Spirit, some of the sadness that had touched Michael's life began to dissipate like clouds over the California coastline burning off under the morning rays of the sun. The bitterness evaporated, and that constant companion, the migraine headache, vanished for the moment. The room seemed a haven of calm, and Michael sensed that others were having a similar experience of peace.

Lonnie was speaking again. "What I'm going to do now is go around and lay hands on you and pray God's Spirit will give you all power." Michael noticed a few people dropping to their knees. A new worry caused him to fidget: these people were getting pretty emotional. As the speaker made his way around the room the weeping became audible. Some were raising their hands, some were singing snatches of a chorus, still others were speaking in a language Michael didn't understand. He really had no idea what was happening, but he was pretty sure he didn't want any part of it. Maybe he ought to be leaving. Then another thought occurred to him: why was he judging these people? Hadn't his behavior been a lot worse than theirs? Hadn't he gone out to Yucca Valley with a bunch of weirdos and waited for spaceships until all hours of the night?

The leader came by and prayed with the person nearest him. Michael was the only one left he had not spoken to. Now he was looking at him: "I'm going to pray for you," he said.

The murmuring and sobbing had increased. "I'm kinda frightened," Michael confessed. "I don't understand what's going on."

"Well, I'm just going to lay hands on you, and if you want to worship God, just go ahead."

Michael shook his head. He didn't like strange, long-haired men touching him! "I don't know one thing you're talking about, but I do love God and I want to serve Him, and I do believe I'm saved tonight."

The man closed his eyes and placed his hands on Michael's forehead. At that moment it seemed as if the heavens opened and a shower of love cascaded down upon him. It came down so strongly that he couldn't stand, but went on his knees and wept like a baby. Then came a sensation of inexpressible warmth, as if everything, even the outer reaches of space and the black holes of the universe, were filled with the glow of God's love. The peace Michael felt was total. He no longer held any grudges; the chips on his shoulder were gone; all his hassles were history. Whatever it was that had enveloped him, it came with awesome power, and he recognized in it the immensity of divine love.

When the Beatles sang, "All you need is love," they were looking for it without knowing what it was. For Michael, at last the mystery was unlocked. He knew from the bottom of his heart that he had been welcomed into the kingdom of love.

For all his interest in other people, and particularly in members of the opposite sex, Michael had never been a demonstrative person. Yet in that little classroom, on his knees, he lifted his hands to God and began speaking. He felt as if his spirit had just been released into the Holy Spirit. The name "Jesus" passed his lips, the "name which is above every name" (Phil. 2:9), the one expression that made sense of the whole creation.

It was as if Michael had been crawling through the weeds and brambles of all the different religions with their gurus, their messiahs, their limousines, and their Mickey Mouse spirits and incantations and had come out on a grassy clearing where the sun was beaming down. Here song thrushes were trilling, tiny forget-me-nots were blooming, and everything with breath was praising the Lord until the love of God seemed overwhelming.

This was truth. This was the pure flame of the gospel of Christ. "For God so loved the world that He gave His only begotten Son, that whoever believes in Him should not perish but have everlasting life" (John 3:16).

As in a dream, Michael saw again the German woman at the farm in Oregon who taught him to read the Bible as a little boy...the Baptist Sunday school teacher who wept at his first confession of Christ...the prayer chapel in the Grotto...a man who saw him reading a book about yoga and handed him a Gideon New Testament...and Jesus. Jesus whom he had seen just before the explosion took

Michael's parents, Wilbur and Ruth MacIntosh, in 1943.

Michael as a 9-year-old Cub Scout in 1953.

The start of Michael's love of fast cars—at age 2½ in 1946.

Michael (right) with his brothers Kent (center) and David (left, with baby son), in December 1958.

Dancing with an early crush at age 13 in 1957.

In uniform as a member of the Army Reserve at age 18 in 1962.

Newlyweds Michael and Sandy with her parents, Wilfrid and Dorothy Riddet, at a reception in the summer of 1966.

With Melinda, the first baby, and a statue of Buddha in 1967.

Michael and Sandy's second wedding in Calvary Chapel, 1971.

Giving his testimony in Rizal stadium, Manila, the Philippines, in 1973

Part of the crowd waiting for the next service at Horizon Christian Fellowship downtown at the old North Park theater, 1982.

Michael preaching during a Communion service in the North Park Church, 1982.

Baptizing a new Christian in the ocean in Hawaii, 1983.

With his pastor and mentor, Chuck Smith, in 1983.

Preaching on the beach in San Diego, 1981.

Bill Goodrich and Michael delivering food and medicine in Poland, 1982. (photo by Dan Wooding)

Michael and team with Spanish-speaking pastors in Mexico City, 1983.

Michael and Sandy at the Great Wall of China, 1980.

Michael and Sandy
as they appear
today, in 1984.

place inside his head that terrible night at Ron's place. Jesus who said to him, "Michael, when the first nail went into My hand, and My blood was shed, your sins were forgiven. You have to receive that and believe it in your heart."

But he didn't—until tonight.

The meeting was over. One by one people were leaving the Sunday school room; the regular evening meeting had long since been dismissed. Michael pedaled his way back to Huntington Beach, stopping at traffic lights and looking up at the stars. "God," he prayed, "You saved me. I'm Yours. I can't believe it!" His heart pounded not from exertion but from elation. Faster and faster he pumped his legs. "What happened?" kept coming to his lips. "What happened, Lord? It's so real and so simple. Wow!"

He reached his house and ran up to the front door filled with the love of God, on fire with the glad tidings of great joy. In the kitchen some of his roommates were sitting, smoking, enjoying a few beers, and discussing rather warmly the future of America's middle class in a revolutionized Marxist society.

"Hey, you guys," exclaimed Michael, "you've got to learn about Jesus Christ and the Holy Spirit. Jesus Christ is coming back and you've got to be born again!"

They stared at him. Smiles appeared, but the discussion continued. They could not comprehend the momentous revolution that had just occurred in Michael's life.

# 15

# Come Off It, Mike!

*Life is not merely being alive, but being well.*
Martial

"Don't tell me, Mike! You got yourself into all those religions, and now you're living in a hippie commune and you try to give me Jesus. Come off it!"

"This is different, Sandy. You've got to believe me. Jesus Christ is the Lord and you've got to accept Him. Don't you see? This is for real."

"I don't want to hear it. You sound crazy; in fact, you're nuttier than you were before. I don't want you coming around bothering me or the kids anymore."

"Sandy," Michael tried again, "you don't understand."

"I understand all right. I was raised a Methodist and have been one all my life. I know more about it than you'll ever know, and it's just not interesting to me."

"Let me just share this with you from the Word—"

"No! I've bought too much from you already. You've always got something new on the string, and usually you've managed to drag me into it. Have you forgotten that you got me a mantra that was supposed to be in alignment with my soul's vibrations?"

"That was before—"

"Don't talk to me about it. It's great for you, that's fine."

Sandra's ire was up. She was in her last semester at Long Beach State, doing student teaching and working for her credentials. The night Michael arrived, she was struggling with a term paper on Keats's poetry and getting ready for a quiz on Hamlet. And here he arrived with this new thing, this Jesus thing.

But now Michael was weeping, and as always Sandra was touched. "Come here," she said. "Let's talk about it." But her ex-husband's effort to win her to his views got nowhere. As he drove disconsolately back to Costa Mesa in his recently repaired car, he vowed that as she had been the chief victim of his disarray, Sandra would now become the centerpiece of his intercessory life. His prayer was not that she would return to him, but that God would touch her life as He had touched his, and that she and the children would soon belong to Christ.

"Dear God, save my family!"

Michael had stopped smoking and drinking and had become a Bible-reading, churchgoing Christian. He took a new interest in his academic courses. At college he became more intimate with Henry Cutrona and his friends. Together they would sit on the steps outside the classroom buildings and read the Bible; cool, hip Michael was now one of those who carried his Bible around the campus.

The church board at Calvary Chapel, conscious that many of the rootless young people who flocked to their services were homeless and destitute, rented a two-story house on Newport Avenue. Pastor Chuck Smith announced at a Wednesday evening prayer meeting that this house would be used as living quarters for Christians, and he introduced Edward Smith as the new elder in charge. After the service, Michael was one of the young men who approached Smith and told him he was looking for a roof over his head.

"I want a place where I can grow in the Lord," Michael said. Smith assured him he would be welcome at the "Christian commune," as the house came to be known. A few days later, Michael showed up at the house in his '48 Buick woody, which was crammed with his records and everything else he possessed, including Arnold. Smith had rounded up a crew to clean out the place, which had been used for pot parties and was in a mess. But Michael asked them to keep an eye on his car and took Arnold and went off and enjoyed himself. He came back a week later when the place was clean and said he was now ready to move in.

The change of address was not without significance. He was leaving the Students for a Democratic Society for "Mansion Messiah," which was the new name Edward Smith gave to the commune. Sandra drove by one day to take a look at the place and saw some young girls carrying in their suitcases. She thought, *Uh huh. I've been through this before with him. This is just Michael's lifestyle, but he has put another name on it.* She was sure it was some kind of hippie, free-sex arrangement.

As for Michael, he continued to be zealous in his efforts to evangelize Sandra. To her he seemed as intense and up-in-another-world about it as he had been about everything else. He hammered away at her on the telephone and asked her to dinner repeatedly until finally she accepted and went to Mansion Messiah. She was surprised at the appearance of the people—they were all so nice looking and spoke so softly. And she was curious. She went back a few times, and even though she was skeptical about Michael's new religion, she couldn't deny that he was looking much better.

This man, who had tried everything and whom no

amount of love or dedication on Sandra's part could change one iota, was beginning to get well. She was astounded. She kept reminding him how he had taken her into the Eastern religions; and when she did, he simply wept. But when she learned that he had sold the woody and given the money to the commune, she informed him that she thought his money could better have gone to the support of his kids.

At first Michael continued to experience LSD flashes, and migraine headaches were plaguing him daily. But shortly after moving into Mansion Messiah he attended a Saturday evening men's prayer meeting at Calvary Chapel and heard a young man who was suffering from seizures ask for prayer. Later in the evening the young man stated publicly that God had healed him. Michael sat thinking, *My case isn't nearly as extreme as his. I just have a psychological condition, but how I wish I could be normal again! I know now I never will be.*

At that moment it seemed that the Lord said to him, "I can heal you." Michael's reaction was to stand and address Pastor Chuck Smith (who hardly knew him) and the elders of the church, who had just been praying with the other young man. Briefly Michael related the story of his descent into the drug culture, the horrible trip, the explosion, the feeling that the left side of his face was missing, the ensuing psychotherapy, the continuing acid flashes and headaches, the uncertainty as to whether he was alive or dead. He then requested prayer and was told to be seated. Pastor Chuck proceeded to anoint him with oil. The elders, all businessmen and "establishment types," gathered around and listened as their pastor read from the fifth chapter of James: "Is anyone among you sick? Let him call for the elders of the church, and let them pray over him, anointing him with oil in the name of the Lord. And the prayer of faith will save the sick, and the

Lord will raise him up. And if he has committed sins, he will be forgiven."

Michael sat with his eyes closed as one of the men laid a hand on his head. He felt a warm, gentle touch, like a mild electrical charge that went from the left side of his head to the right; and in an instant he knew that his mind was back, that he was normal. A verse came to him: "God has not given us a spirit of fear, but of power and of love and of a sound mind" (2 Tim. 1:7). He fell out of the chair on his face and began weeping. He had resigned himself to the idea that he would be mentally crippled for the rest of his life, and yet now he had the assurance that he was well. He thanked God and glorified His name, finding it almost too good to be believable. His sense of the love of God was overwhelming. And in the ecstasy of that moment, the thought came to him that others could be healed, too; that people, knowing what had happened to him, would ask God to heal their sons and daughters; that others in a condition as hopeless as his would take heart, pray to God, and be made whole.

# 16

# The Gospel Swamp

*A span of life is nothing. But the man who lives that
span, he is something.*
Chaim Potok, *The Chosen*

"The Pied Piper of the Jesus Generation," "the spiritual
father to lost youth," "the pastor of the world's most unusual church"—many titles were given to Charles Smith,
pastor of Calvary Chapel in Costa Mesa, California, during the 1970s. For Michael MacIntosh, who had never
really known a father, the man was an awesome figure to
be revered at a distance; and at the same time he was a
magnet. For the next five years Chuck Smith, as he was
universally called, was to become the most important person in Michael's life. Out of a world filled with con men
and quacks, here at last he found a plain, unassuming person who seemed to have neither pretense nor guile. With
his stocky frame, the fringe around his handsome bald
head, the disarming smile, the twinkle in his eye, and his
astonishing knowledge of the Bible, Chuck Smith actually
seemed to know what was going on. When he opened his
Bible, a mantle of divine authority such as Michael could
not question descended upon him. To shake hands with
him seemed a little like shaking hands with God.

What was true for Michael was also true for thousands of young men and women, many of whom had not been inside a church in years, if ever. In the early 1970s they came swarming into the church parking lot, dropping their joints outside, slumping into the pews, sticking their bare toes through the communion cup holders, and pouring their drugs down the church toilet. For them Costa Mesa was the New Jerusalem, and Chuck Smith was a new John the Baptist. Richard Ostling described the pastor for *Time* magazine: "Smith is a Bible teacher, not an old-style hell-fire and brimstone evangelist or a psychoanalyst. He is actually a balding Everyman. But he knows the traumas and failures of fragmenting society and family life, and the apocalyptic feeling that today assails many Americans" (Dec. 26, 1977).

Such a man hardly seems to have been a likely candidate to teach the "kandy-kolored tangerine-flake electric kool-aid acid generation" that produced the hippies, the flower children, and the Jesus freaks. Charles Ward Smith started out to become a neurosurgeon, and in high school his outside reading consisted of books on the brain. Things were realigned for him at a Foursquare church youth retreat in the San Bernardino mountains, and he began attending Bible classes at a church college in Los Angeles. By the time he was twenty years old, he was out of school and pastoring a church in Prescott, Arizona, at a salary of fifteen dollars a week. By the year 1963 Smith had spent seventeen years in the ministry, was thirty-seven years old, and felt totally discouraged. Instead of growing, he found his congregations were actually shrinking. He was sick of what he called "the stifling, restrictive role I was required to play" as a clergyman. Finally he resigned from his denomination's ministry and went into the building trade.

During his last pastorate in southern California, Smith

had begun teaching the Bible in people's homes, evoking a positive response that was a welcome relief after the futility he experienced in church on Sundays. This home study activity he pursued, and he was invited to nearby communities to start new classes. He found that in a private house or apartment he could expound God's Word—and answer questions—for up to two hours, with the complete attention of his audience. Inevitably churches grew out of those Bible studies. After two years, he gave up working on houses and cleaning carpets and accepted a call to return to an independent church ministry. A small congregation located in a part of Costa Mesa known as "the gospel swamp" wanted his services, or at least part of it did. The vote was thirteen to twelve. Smith's wife, Kay, did not find the call convincing since she was rearing a family of four and he was proposing to leave a growing congregation of two hundred.

The phenomenal growth of Calvary Chapel, as the church was called, has yet to be fully documented. Teaching instead of preaching proved to be a popular switch. Sunday morning attendance grew steadily for a while, then took off. Calvary Chapel became the fountainhead of what was happening all along the West Coast as thousands of youths turned their backs on the drug scene and sought refuge in Jesus. They became known as "Jesus people," and their notoriety became contagious as the word spread eastward. At Calvary Chapel the word was: you don't have to be "different," you can come as you are. Chuck Smith went out of his way to befriend hippies, to listen to them and try to understand them. He told his congregation: "Our church lost a whole generation of young people with a negative, no-movie, no-dance gospel. Let us at Calvary not be guilty of the same mistake. Instead, let us trust God and emphasize the work of the

Holy Spirit within individual lives. We want change to come from inside out."

Unconsciously, perhaps, Calvary Chapel was gearing up for a worldwide ministry, but at the moment the chief attraction was the teaching of Pastor Chuck. It might be a Psalm or Luke or Romans or 1 John he was expounding, but the principles and the pattern were the same. People opened their Bibles and followed his exegesis, and the sheep were fed. To walk into Calvary Chapel as Michael did that night in 1970 was to see a unique assortment of headbands, embroidered shirts, jeans, beards, long skirts, and long hair; but what you saw was nothing compared to what you heard. New musical groups were springing into existence, new choruses were being written and sung, guitars were twanging, and hour after hour drums were sounding the beat. The atmosphere was congenial to the Jesus generation; people said it was great.

Then came the announcement about the opening of the first "Christian commune," and within a few days Michael moved in. There was still, in Chuck Smith's view, a spaciness about him, a vagueness and an inability to concentrate on one subject. He was, in fact, a pool of ignorance on the subject of the Christian life; and yet for the first time in a long while Michael was comfortable. He felt he had found home.

# 17

# Mansion Messiah

*The grace of God makes a man godly,
and then proceeds to make him manly.*
Henrietta Mears

Edward Tracy Smith was only three-and-one-half months old "in the Lord" when Pastor Chuck Smith tapped him to be elder in charge of Calvary Chapel's new Christian commune. He was branch manager of a fiberglass-weaving company, was divorced from his wife, and had a serious drinking problem before a business associate took him to Calvary Chapel. There, as Ed tells it, "I met the Lord." He also met the pastor, and Chuck Smith was impressed with this handsome, twenty-nine-year-old convert who looked as if he had just stepped out of the Los Angeles Rams locker room. He stood six feet four inches and weighed 235 pounds.

By his own frank admission at the time of his appointment, Ed Smith was "not too bright in the Word," but he knew something about human nature. He knew what a disorganized lifestyle had done to him, and he determined that Mansion Messiah would become a productive training base for young Christians. If the Christian life was what the Bible said it was, a warfare, then his job was to regiment and discipline the raw troops. Under his direction the old house underwent a complete renovation. New plumbing was put in, repairs were made, rooms were painted, and the garage was turned into a bedroom. Everything was made spic and span, and within a short while some forty people had moved in.

One primary rule dominated the operation of Mansion Messiah: every person who crossed the threshold was to be confronted with the love and the claims of the Lord Jesus Christ. Ed Smith believed that if people came to the home, it was because God sent them; therefore, if God wanted them to receive something, it was his job and the job of his colleagues to deliver it. The colleagues got the message. When a telephone company representative came to collect the money from the pay phone under the staircase, he was on his way out the door when someone asked, "Has anybody shared with him?"

"Gee, I don't think so," said Ed.

By the time the man reached his truck, three brothers were ministering to him, preaching to him and, in the language of the day, "watching God work." The man and his whole family soon came to dinner at the mansion and started attending Calvary Chapel.

Others got the same treatment. The police showed up, as hippie communes did not enjoy a good reputation among southern California law officers. But at Mansion Messiah the officers were witnessed to, and it was not long before they began stopping by for coffee. On weekends the place was turned into what became known as an "evangelistic hangout" (a new word in the Christian lexicon). As many as two hundred people would crowd the house. Many of them were drifters brought in by the residents who found them lying on Newport Beach. All were welcomed, fed, and told about Jesus. They were given a place to sleep; if the bunks were full, they stretched out on the floor, in hallways, or in the backyard.

Another rule Ed Smith laid down was that everyone studied the Bible. Mansion Messiah was to be no crash pad. It was Bible study for an hour, morning, noon, and night; and in addition each resident was expected to have his personal Bible study. No radios, television, newspapers, or magazines were allowed in the house—just the Bible. Sometimes the residents would stay up until midnight studying chapters and memorizing verses. Everybody was young in the faith; nobody knew Hebrew or Greek, so the interpretation of the text was apt to be curious, if not downright wrong. But the love was there, the motivation was unimpeachable and the determination very strong. It was verse by verse, line by line, precept upon precept, memorize and underline, read and study, listen and learn, pray and study some more.

For most Christians, reading the Bible is a duty and a discipline. For these guys and girls it was top sirloin, spuds, and gravy served on a warm platter after a long fast. No abbot enforced a monastic rule, no hair shirts were issued, but Ed Smith stood ready to kick the tail end of any goldbrick off the front porch if he wasn't there to get to know the Lord and do his bit. You want to stay here? You get into the Bible.

Ed had still another rule that he took straight out of Thessalonians: everybody worked. The Mansion had to be self-supporting, for Calvary Chapel contributed nothing but prayers. The people who lived there took jobs and turned in their earnings to the house. If they were coming off drugs and still unfit to work outside, they were kept busy around the place, planting a vegetable garden, building bunk beds, working in the kitchen, and keeping the place neat and tidy. Some of the fellows worked in grocery stores and talked the managers into leaving dented cans and day-old milk and bread out back for them instead of throwing it all into the dumpsters. Strangers were welcomed for a night or two, and if they were hurting badly they were helped; but if they didn't want to give their hearts to Christ, study the Bible, and do some work, they were invited to move on. Most of the live-ins had been on the streets and could discern whether a person was looking for help or just freeloading and bumming around town.

In the rooming arrangements Ed enforced the strictest discipline. Upstairs was upstairs and downstairs was downstairs. Any hanky-panky, any infraction in the area of man-woman relationships was dealt with severely, for the house lived by a stern code. Usually it meant immediate dismissal. Actually the number of problems in that area that surfaced was minimal, although to the world outside the fact was difficult to accept.

For Michael MacIntosh, life in a Christian commune was a brand-new experience. It was to be the only Bible college and theological seminary he would ever know. Mansion Messiah became an anchor for him and made him strong in the Scriptures. It gave him the first taste of discipline that he was able to accept. He still carried seeds of rebellion, but he saw that Ed Smith was a well-organized individual and that the discipline he enforced was always couched in love. What appealed most to him about the place and its people was the camaraderie and the cheerful atmosphere. Like the early followers of Francis of Assisi, they laughed a lot. He noticed all the residents seemed to have a common purpose. They were all trying to learn the Word of God and were working to support each other.

When he first came to the commune Michael was not well enough to do much work; but as he grew stronger, and people came to the house looking for short-term laborers, he went out on assignments. He repossessed furniture and delivered it to a nearby auctioneer; he also cut down eucalyptus trees around an orange grove. Ed Smith took an instant liking to him, sensing that their backgrounds were not too dissimilar. As Michael began to show responsibility in the tasks assigned him, Ed gave him supervisory tasks and eventually appointed him a deacon. That appointment afterward gave Ed qualms; he wasn't sure that God was in it. On one occasion while they were eating breakfast in the kitchen and discussing some subject or other, Michael became upset.

"I thought we were here to talk about the Lord," he said.

"We're here to grow up in the Lord," Ed told him. "You've got to give us time."

Michael also had big ideas, or as the current vocabulary would have it, "great vision." He wanted to take off for Hollywood. He wanted to go to London, not to be the fifth Beatle any more, but to minister to the other four. Ed had to sit down and explain that all of them were going through a time of preparation, that God was the One who was in charge. "When God calls you to something, God prepares you for that something." Meanwhile there was a work order to be filled, and he had better find somebody to do it or do it himself.

On one occasion, two hundred people gathered for a potluck supper at the house, and Michael gave up his seat to one of the visitors and went outside. After the meal Ed Smith began to teach the Bible lesson. He was sitting next to the living room window with people jammed all around him when suddenly the window opened and Michael was there, standing in the flower bed. "Don't forget to tell them about the love of God!" he said, grinning.

It was evident that God had touched Michael in the area of love, because that was all he wanted to talk about. But he was not alone; the whole household seemed to be overtaken with the love of God. "When you depart from the

Word of God," Ed warned them, "the concept of love becomes wishy-washy. It takes on emotional overtones and it does not include the discipline that God has in His Word. We are to express our love in the context of the Bible. When we see people doing what is wrong, we are to confront them with true, godly love, and show them that they must live according to the Scriptures to have fulfilled lives, that what they are saying is not what the Bible says. But we are to restore them in a spirit of meekness, and when we do, they will come looking for it."

The young men and women who came to Mansion Messiah were often from above-average income homes. They said their parents had given them so many things they considered it a farce. The gifts conveyed no reality to them. The parents thought they could express their love with material goods, but it left their children confused. Then they listened to Timothy Leary telling them to get loaded and find utopia, and they tried it and found out it was a lie.

Such was their condition when they came to Calvary Chapel and Mansion Messiah, and the results were astounding. "God brought forth tremendous fruit in that house," says Ed Smith. "No one soul was responsible for it, for the Holy Spirit was simply pouring out the love of God upon that place." One of the greatest difficulties the leaders had was staying with the new converts, some of whom attempted to lead others to Christ two days after they were saved. Problems often resulted. And yet those connected with the work contend that statistically Mansion Messiah had one of the highest ratios of success and longevity that any rehabilitation program has ever seen. The reason, they say, was that the love of God was manifested, and God was worshiped and studied.

Michael's leadership qualities began to emerge when a rebellion broke out in the house. Ed learned that one of his deacons was smoking marijuana and informed him he could no longer be a deacon. Michael, not knowing all the facts, sided with the accused and said, "If he goes, I go." Ed went off to work. He received a telephone call from Michael that afternoon.

"God is really doing a heavy number here," he said. "You'd better get home. Eleven people are ready to move out."

"That's the way it is," said Ed. "Just relax."

But by the time Ed got home, Michael had learned the truth and decided his loyalty lay with the man in authority. It was a first for the long-time rebel, and it worked. Four people ended up leaving in the commotion, but more important, Michael's leadership was established. From that time on he began to assume more responsibility. When an older man came into the house while Ed was away and began spewing false doctrine, saying that a child could not come to Jesus, Michael challenged him, declaring that he had received Christ when he was eleven years old, even though he did not follow Him then.

When the man persisted, Michael said to him, "I know you're off-the-wall. What you're saying is wrong, and you're not to talk about it in this house."

The older man stared at him. "Who do you think you are?"

"I'm asking you to leave," Michael replied. The man did, but he left Michael shaken. When Ed Smith returned and learned about it, he said, "Your spiritual discernment was correct. That man has given Chuck Smith trouble. If I had been here he never would have come across our front porch."

A major problem facing the residents of Mansion Messiah was indebtedness. Many of them had run up large bills and when Ed Smith called for an accounting and added them up, they came to nearly seven thousand dollars. Ed informed each one that he was to write a check every week for five or ten dollars on each of the bills owed. He himself telephoned the creditors to make sure the money was getting to the right place. He knew the kids were pretty good con artists and had learned how to avoid responsibility. Now the Lord was teaching them His way. The debtors would call up individuals whom they had ripped off and make some arrangement. Then they prayed that God would bring in the money. But most of the creditors, when they heard about the good news of Jesus Christ and what he had done in their lives, just tore up the bills. The seven thousand dollar debt was cut in less than half, which added considerably to the faith of the young people.

Michael was so deeply in debt that he was considering bankruptcy. Among other bills, he owed his psychologist a hundred dollars. According to plan, he wrote him a ten-dollar check and took it to his office; but when he tried to slip it under the door, the door opened and there was his doctor looking at him.

"Come in, Mike," he said. "How are you doing?"

"Well, it's like this," said Michael, and he reeled off what Jesus Christ had done in his life.

The doctor listened and said, "You don't need to give me this ten dollars."

"Oh, yes, I do," protested Michael. "You put it out for collection, and if I pay them, you only get 50 percent."

"You don't understand," said the therapist. "You don't have any bill with me at all!"

During the five months that Michael stayed at Mansion Messiah, he saw people being saved in droves. So many were converted that Calvary Chapel opened up a second commune and sent leaders from Mansion Messiah to take charge. But the real key to the commune's astonishing ministry to a needy element of society was not its witness-

ing or its evangelism or its discipline; the real key was
prayer. Prayer saturated everything that was done. Telephone calls ended in prayer. Before a car or a truck would
start, someone offered prayer. Small items, big enter-
prises, everything was taken to the Lord for guidance and
direction—and for enablement. Did they need lumber for
some more bunk beds? The petition was laid on the dining
room table and prayed over. That same night Ed Smith attended the men's prayer meeting at Calvary Chapel, and a
man spoke to him:

"Do you need any wood up there?"

"Yes, we could use some two-by-fours."

"How many?"

"About a hundred and fifty."

"Well, I can let you have a hundred and fifty two-by-
sixes."

Obviously, Smith's design was off; the Lord wanted the
bunks made stronger, so he provided the two-by-sixes.

Ed Smith started out to regiment the troops and prepare them for the spiritual warfare every true Christian
must face. The message that Michael took away from
Mansion Messiah after five months in boot camp was
God's word to the prophet Joel: "Blow the trumpet in
Zion…for the day of the LORD is coming"! (2:1). Armaged-
don is at hand, and it is not another war-games exercise.
The time is ripe; the need is urgent. Get ready. Bring them
in before it is too late. Raise up an army and go to battle!

# 18

# Return of the Dragon

*Hope deferred makes the heart sick,
but when the desire comes, it is a tree of life.*
Proverbs 13:12

One day toward the end of his stay at Mansion Messiah, Michael telephoned Sandra: "They're having a picnic and hot dog roast on the beach at Corona del Mar Saturday," he said.

"Oh, yeah?"

"Yeah. A great musical group will be there. Thought you might like to join them."

"Are you going?"

"No, I can't. Got to prepare for a Bible study. But you go. I know you'll like it."

She wasn't sure. But a cousin of Sandra's was in town, an Idaho football coach, and she talked to him about it. He offered to go with her. Saturday came, and when they arrived at the beach Sandra blinked her eyes at what she saw. The whole area was overrun with people—over two thousand of them, all young—and Love Song was filling the air with electric guitar music. To Sandra the sights and sounds coming from the beach were fascinating. She could feel the atmosphere charged with emotion and love, and it cut her to the heart. *So this must be what Michael's always talking about,* she thought. *If it's real, then I have to admit he is right. This guy who had so many needs and was so broken has found an answer that works.*

And now Sandra had to face her own life. She had thought she had it all together as a proper young woman and a good mother. She was trying hard and studying hard, and she had worked out what she considered a sensible and satisfying plan for her life. But it dawned on her that day that her need was as great as Michael's. She could see the emptiness inside herself, and it was terribly humiliating. Michael had always been "sick Michael," and she had always been "well Sandy." *Yes, this was what Michael needed*, she thought, and then it was like a brick falling on her: *This is what I need, even though I have felt so complete up till now.*

She was standing with her cousin, and their mouths were literally hanging open. Then a lot of people stood up and clambered over the rocks and went down into the cove of the Pacific Ocean to be baptized. Sandra started down and got into line with them.

"What are you doing?" asked her cousin as she made her move.

"I have to get baptized," she told him.

Eventually she found herself standing alongside a tall young man with long blond hair. She had no idea who he was, never having seen him before.

"I have to do this," she said to him.

"Are you born again?" he asked her.

"I don't think so."

"Well, then, let's pray."

He held her hands and they prayed, and Sandra asked the Lord into her heart. Then she went out into the water and was baptized. The man who baptized her was the same man whose message had led Michael to Christ. She waded back to the beach dripping wet. No towels were provided. She found her cousin standing and waiting for her. It seemed something had happened to him, too. They just fell into each other's arms. Then they got into his car and drove over to the commune where Michael was staying. It was nine o'clock at night when Michael answered the knock. There was his ex-wife, dripping wet and smiling from ear to ear with the glow of love on her. He couldn't believe it. He could barely speak he was so touched. She said to him, "You have really found the truth this time!" And they both cried.

In the two years since the divorce, both Michael and Sandra had been dating other people. Now it seemed logical that they should get married again, but it didn't happen. Sandra continued her studies at Long Beach and began worshiping at Calvary Chapel. She met new Christian friends and studied the Bible as she had never studied it before. The man she was dating went to church with her and became a Christian.

Ed Smith was just leaving Mansion Messiah for the Laundromat one day with one of the "sisters" (as the female residents were called) and a huge load of soiled laundry, when Sandra dropped by.

"Can I come along?" she asked.

"Sure."

During the trip she managed to get Smith alone. "Well, Ed," she asked, "do you think that God can put people back together?"

"Certainly," he replied.

"But do you think it would be all right if Michael and I did it?"

"It would be very much all right if God brought you both to that place of relationship. I don't put anything past Him."

Michael's first break came in October. The owner of the defunct Community Playhouse in Glendale, just north of Los Angeles, paid a visit to Calvary Chapel and was so impressed by its ministry to youth that she spoke to Pastor Chuck. "Can't you get something going for our kids up there? They're running wild. You can have my theater if you want."

Smith investigated the place, accepted the offer, and appointed one of his trainees, Randy Morich, to head the work. By combing the town, Randy rounded up eight young fellows, including Michael, to assist him.

The Glendale Playhouse was a theater in the round that seated 140 persons. Morich turned its dressing rooms into dormitories and moved into a house on the back of the property with his wife, Patty.

For Michael it was the end of an epoch. For five months the Bible had been the only book he had held in his hands. Now boot camp was over, and he was relocating on the staging area. Ed Smith hated to see Mike move his stuff out of Mansion Messiah, but he was glad, too, because he knew the Lord was calling Michael to a new ministry.

Michael was driven to Glendale, where he unrolled a sleeping bag on the floor of one of the dressing rooms. The work started from scratch. They were out on the street, talking to people, distributing handbills, inviting folks to a Bible study. The first night five showed up. The next night eight. The praying and witnessing went on, and Calvary Chapel sent some musicians to hold a concert. Within thirty days the theater was overflowing with two hundred people. Someone knew Pat Boone, and he showed up and brought his four daughters who sang. Things were booming in Glendale. Michael and his colleagues were sharing their testimonies at the meetings and praying with inquirers. But Michael was also praying for a mattress; the wooden floor of the dressing room was getting harder each night. After six weeks, what should arrive on a moving van driven by Tony and Mary Laddadio of Calvary Chapel but a thick mattress, plus box spring and frame, plus sheets and a pillow! *A bed!* thought Michael. *Wow! I'm a real person again!* And God taught him how to pray for basic necessities.

Once, when he drew the assignment of cleaning the rest rooms, he wondered if it wasn't time to reevaluate his situation. As he got on his knees and scrubbed the toilet bowls, he reflected, *The time is short, right? I ought to be out preaching, saving souls on their way to hell, filling stadiums like Billy Graham, right?* And where was he? On his hunkers, communing with the urinal cakes. But even while he scrubbed, a familiar tune came floating into the bathroom over the intercom. It was from the new Love Song album:

> Hey, have you lost the feeling?
> Don't you hear the music any more?
> Hey, have you tried to listen
> But you thought you'd heard the song before?
> Jesus puts the song in our hearts...[1]

As Michael listened, the Holy Spirit's love began to catch up with the words to the song. In the midst of his grumbling and complaining the peace of the Lord was suddenly there in that bathroom as he was on his knees with his hand in the toilet bowl. At that instant the Lord showed him that if he could just be content with Him in whatever he did, he could have the same blessing that Billy Graham had standing in his pulpit in front of fifty thousand people. He realized as a young Christian a great

---

[1]From the song "Jesus Puts the Song in Our Hearts" by Fred Field and Chuck Girard, ©1970 Dunamis Music/ASCAP. Used by permission. All rights reserved.

spiritual truth: "Godliness with contentment is great gain" (1 Tim. 6:6). He was experiencing so much of the Lord's presence at that moment that he concluded, *If this is what He has called me to do, I'd better do it!*

It was Thanksgiving Day 1970. Michael was scheduled to preach in the theater, and Randy and Patty Morich invited Sandra to come and hear him. She did her best, but the Santa Ana freeway was jammed, and she was four hours late. Even so, as she parked in the pastor's driveway she had a feeling of anticipation. Something was in the air. She was not planning to marry Michael; she had an understanding with her boyfriend. But she sensed the Lord telling her that she had to be open to what He was going to do, that something was about to happen.

She had brought Mindi and David, and the reunion was a happy one. They had dinner in the Morich home and afterward, as she was putting the children in the car to drive back to Tustin, Michael kept his hand on the edge of the car door and looked at her. Then he said, "I think God wants us to get married again."

"Yeah," said Sandra, "I know. I do, too." And she drove off with the children.

Michael stared after her. *What did I say?* Sandra had every reason to hate his guts. She had every right to be filled with bitterness. He could hardly wait until she reached home before he was on the telephone. "What did we just say? What's going on?" They agreed to pray about it. If God wanted them to get together again, He would have to do it. There was no way they could do it. Other people were now involved. What should they do, then? Whom should they talk to?

Chuck Smith.

"There's no reason why you shouldn't remarry," Chuck told Sandra. "You have two fine children, and you both know the Lord. You've made mistakes, but your past is gone."

The Riddets.

The answer there was no. They were completely against it. It was *déjà vu*, the return of the dragon. After all, they had underwritten Sandra's expenses all the way through school, had provided for her and her children, and could see light at last at the end of the tunnel as their daughter was getting ready to graduate and test her wings. And now here she was calling them on the telephone and saying, "I've got to marry this man again!" and claiming the "got to" was not her idea, but God's.

And what about Michael? they asked. He had no job and no future. He was in some kind of a teaching ministry with young people in Glendale that provided only room and board. He was contributing nothing to the support of the children. What was different about the situation this time? What made him a better risk than he was in Las Vegas? She had thrown herself away once. That ought to be enough.

Every time Sandra talked on the telephone with her mother the conversation would end in tears, with her mother crying, "How can you do this?"

When she told Michael about it, his response was: "They have every right to be against it, considering everything. But tell your mother that God is in this, and that He is going to bring so much love and fruit out of this that we are all going to love each other more and we are all going to be happy together."

Sandra called back and told her mother that, and it stopped the tears. "O.K.," she said, "how can I argue with that?" But the doubts remained.

# 19

# Love Song

*I am my beloved's, and my beloved is mine.*
Song of Solomon 6:3

The time had come to look for a job.

Bible study was great, street witnessing was exciting, but a wife and two hungry kids were something else. Michael spoke to Chuck Smith about it, and Chuck introduced him to Robert Ward, an elder in his church and president of a burglar alarm company. It took four interviews, but he finally landed a job as salesman and was given the territory of Los Angeles. That meant another move. The Christmas season approached, and Michael was telephoning his ex-wife every day and writing her love letters.

Sandra did a lot of praying. As she drove to Long Beach to her classes at the university, she asked God to give her some sort of assurance that she and this man, who had caused her so much emotional agony, could make it together. They had been so far apart. It was as if he had been standing on one rim of the Grand Canyon and she on the other. One day, as she was driving to school, she heard God tell her, "Behold, I make all things new" (Rev. 21:5). It was so real she had to pull off the road and park. From that minute she knew that if God was going to do it, He would make it happen. She told Michael later, "It doesn't matter how I feel about it or how you feel. What I do, I have to do out of obedience, whether I want to or not." But in her heart she really did want to remarry him.

By January both Michael and Sandra had taken care of unfinished business in breaking off their involvements with other people. Then Michael put in a call to Chuck Smith.

"Oh, Chuck, this is Mike MacIntosh."

"How are you doing, Mike?"

"Well, I was wondering if you could marry Sandy and me."

"How about April third?"

"Yeah, O.K. That's fine. Good-bye, Chuck."

For reasons known only to himself, Pastor Chuck had set the wedding date three months away. In the interim Michael had an immediate housing problem; and with no money and nothing else available, he moved into Sandra's Tustin apartment. After all, they had been married, they had two children, and they were to be remarried. So what was the problem? It was that God said no—no to sex, that is.

"The Lord told me that even though we had been married before, we now need to be married in Him," Michael told his former wife. So Sandra slept in one bedroom and Melinda and David in the other, while Michael pulled out the rollaway bed. A friend who lived across the hall knocked on their door one morning at six o'clock; it seems he had tried to start his car and found the battery dead. When Michael answered the door, the friend stared at him and then at the disheveled sheets on the sofa. "What goes on, MacIntosh?"

"I can't sleep with her till we're married."

"But she's your own wife!"

"It's the spiritual principle that matters."

The man shook his head. "I guess you're serious about this Jesus Christ stuff, aren't you?"

Three hundred people gathered on April 3, 1971, for what was perhaps the most unusual marriage ceremony ever conducted in Calvary Chapel. Hippies, beach-bums, car salesmen, Disneyland performers, bartenders, church people, student radicals, Stephens College graduates—all converged to witness the event. The wedding party was made up of the bride's parents, Wilfrid and Dorothy Riddet, who were now California residents; the maid of honor, Betsy Thorsen, who was later to marry the Olympic decathlon champion, Rafer Johnson; the best man, Michael's brother Kent; and the ecstatic flower girl, three-and-a-half-year-old Melinda, child of the bride and groom. The mother of the bridegroom was absent, as was the father. Music was provided by Love Song, headed by Chuck Girard and including Tommy Coomes, Fred Field, and Jay Truax. They were dressed in Levis and open-necked shirts.

Things started normally enough, with Calvary Chapel friends serving as ushers. Dorothy Riddet, mother of the bride, was escorted to her pew. Waiting in an anteroom were Pastor Chuck, the best man, and the bridegroom, the latter wearing brown slacks, a blue shirt, and white sports jacket. Chuck led the two brothers in a brief prayer, and at that moment the Lord put a question to Michael's heart: "What would you like for a wedding present?" He thought of all the people who had come to the nuptials and decided nothing could be better than that all of them should be saved and come to know the Lord. And God spoke to his heart again: "That's your wedding present."

The music began, and the miracle of love seemed to float across the church pews on waves of sound. Chuck

Girard started the weeping himself during their powerful rendition of "Feel the Love." He managed to regain his composure, but then the other musicians began to crack. People in the pews reached for their handkerchiefs. Probably the only dry eyes belonged to the bride's parents and Sandra's two closest girlfriends, who were all too aware of what phase one of her marriage had been like.

Little Melinda now came down the aisle, carrying a bouquet of white daisies Dorothy Riddet had gathered from her Santa Ana backyard. (The Riddets were determined to invest nothing in what they considered not only their daughter's redundancy, but an out-and-out bad deal.) Melinda walked toward her waiting father, intending to show him her flowers, but tripped on her long dress and scattered daisies all over the carpet. From the pews came gasps and titters. Michael stooped to help his daughter pick up her posies, and as he did he began to cry. *This is my daughter*, he thought. *I've got her back*.

Sandra now appeared at the head of the aisle on her father's arm. From the day she was born, Bill Riddet had looked forward to the hour when he would escort his daughter down the aisle at her wedding. Las Vegas seemed to have cheated him out of that thrill, but here he was in a retake! Sandra was attired in a floor-length organdy dress, long-sleeved, Juliet style. This time she was wearing shoes. Her bouquet was made up of roses and ranunculi, also snipped from the Riddet garden. As she walked toward Michael with her father, the bridegroom made a quick assessment of where he stood. *Everything I destroyed*, he thought, *God is giving back to me. Here I am, and by rights I should be dead. But in spite of all the pills I swallowed and all the crazy things I did with my life, I'm healed. This is really what being born again means! God is restoring my whole life to me. I am nothing but a complete salvage operation, a sinner saved by grace.*

By the time Sandra reached him, Michael was crying

again. He stepped forward to take her arm and was so blinded by his tears that he took Bill Riddet's arm instead. Tears were dripping off his chin. Sandra looked at him demurely with just a touch of tenderness. "Where's your happy Jesus face?" she whispered. But Michael was speechless; she had to help him up the three steps to the pulpit platform where, exactly a year before, he had knelt in an empty sanctuary and prayed to God for help.

*I've got to pull myself together*, Michael thought. *I'll watch Pastor Chuck; that's what I'll do. He's solid and steady. I'll watch him and I'll be all right.* He squared his shoulders and faced the minister.

"Dearly beloved," said the pastor in his kindly mellow baritone, "we are gathered here together—" He paused and tears formed in his eyes.

At that moment Michael lost all control and bawled openly. It was a while before the ceremony could go on.

But go on it did: the wedding vows were said, Michael and Sandra were once more husband and wife, Melinda and David had their daddy back, and three hundred people burst into applause and cheers. Since the newlyweds' cash was in short supply, the wedding reception that followed was potluck.

The bride and groom had spent the first night of their first honeymoon sleeping in a Ford Falcon on a street in Santa Barbara. This honeymoon, thanks to a wedding gift from brother Jim Riddet and a collection taken up by fellow employees at Tel-Alarm, they spent at the historic old Hotel del Coronado across the harbor from San Diego. They occupied the cheapest and smallest room in the elegant hostelry, definitely not the VIP suite that was the lodging in the past of presidents McKinley, Theodore and Franklin Roosevelt, King Kalakaua of Hawaii, Emperor Haile Selassie, and the soon-to-be Duchess of Windsor, Mrs. Bessie Wallis Warfield Spencer Simpson.

# 20

# Baling Wire and Chewing Gum

*Many a fellow is praying for rain*
*with his tub the wrong side up.*
Sam P. Jones, Evangelist

Two unique facts about Paul of Tarsus may occasionally be underplayed, if not overlooked, by people who make their living expounding theology. The first is that the famous apostle to the Gentiles received his biblical training in Jerusalem at the feet of one man, the eminent Pharisee, Rabbi Gamaliel (so he informed a crowd in Acts 22:3). The second is that Paul's call to preach the gospel was inextricably woven with his conversion to Jesus Christ. When Paul was still blinded from his Damascus road encounter with his Lord, the Damascus disciple Ananias was informed by the same Lord that Paul was "a chosen vessel to Me, to bear My name before the nations" (Acts 9:15, author's translation).

In many churches today ministerial training begins with the first year of college and continues for seven or eight years, to be climaxed by a seminary degree. The fledgling is exposed to everything from Hebrew to hermeneutics to homiletics, after which he or she is turned out to face the grim reality of the religious market. Unlike most theologues today, but more like the apostle Paul, Michael MacIntosh never saw the inside of a Bible school or theological seminary. Instead he sat under one man for nearly five years. Every minute he could spare, day or night, he spent with Chuck Smith. He watched this man, studied him, followed him more than once through the Bible, observed his preaching and evangelistic methods and his reactions to all kinds of people and situations.

The young man who used to spend time on the beach picking up bottles or just lying around now began to make himself useful at Calvary Chapel. Did some drifter need to be counseled about psychedelic drugs? "Hey, I'll be glad to do it." Was some new Christian wanting to start a home Bible study? "I'll come and teach it." He trailed around after staff members asking them, "How do I get into the ministry? What do you do?" In most churches the answer would have been, "Finish your college work, son, and we'll see you get into our seminary" or "Better put in for a good Bible school." The advice he got at Calvary Chapel was, "Just make yourself available and pray. God will work it out."

The problem was that in 1971 Michael's time wasn't his own. He was supposed to be on the road introducing Orange County and Los Angeles to the unspeakable blessings of burglar alarms. Furthermore, he owed money all over southern California and had been in the financial pits ever since the FBI had been to see him four years earlier about that bogus check he had cashed in Florida on an Oregon bank. In 1969 he went so far as to fill out forms for declaring Chapter 11 bankruptcy and gave them to his brother-in-law, the attorney. But for some reason Jim Riddet put the papers in a drawer and never did file them.

After he was reunited with Sandra and his family, Michael was confirmed more strongly than ever in his calling to a full-time ministry, but with a difference: he wanted the whole world to know the marvel of God's love. Was he personally qualified for such a gigantic undertaking? Why not? Nobody could get by him now. "If their marriage is broken, I can tell them what the Lord did for me. If they've blown their minds with drugs, I can tell them who will put them together. If they are drunks, I can tell them who will dry them out. If they've lost all their money, I can point to the One who will make them fiscally responsible. If they're filled with bitterness, I can tell them how to be filled with the Spirit. If they're tempted, I can tell them about the Great Overcomer. If they have a bad self-image, I can offer them a Christ-image. No matter how weak they are or how many failures they've had, I know that Jesus will love them and forgive them and that He can work a miracle in their lives the way He did for me."

Meanwhile Calvary Chapel had launched a new venture. Some of the young musicians had cut a recording of Christian rock, which they called "The Everlasting Living Jesus Concert." It combined the talents of Love Song, Blessed Hope, Country Faith, and other groups and vocalists. To produce it, Chuck Smith formed a small, subsidiary, nonprofit company which he called "Maranatha! Music." When Michael heard about it he went to Laverne Romaine, a former marine sergeant major who was now assistant to Pastor Chuck. "I feel," he said, "that God is telling me to get this record out for Him."

"Are you a salesman?" asked Romaine dubiously.

"Yeah."

"A good salesman?"

"I was a master salesman for Fiat cars. I can do it."

"Well," said Romaine, "if you plan to do this in the flesh, you won't sell these records, but if God is calling you then they'll sell."

Bob Ward, president of Tel-Alarm, heard what was happening and called Michael into his office. "Mike," he said, "you can't be double-minded and you know it. Either you're working for me or you're working for Maranatha."

It was quite a step for a penurious bridegroom of two months who was now head of a family of four, but he took it. In June of 1971 Michael switched from alarm squeals to sacred music. First he rustled two shoe boxes, one to hold receipts and the other the consignment money. Then he stacked his garage with record supplies and started making the rounds of Christian bookstores in the surrounding counties. He was driving a sixty-five dollar 1961 Plymouth Valiant that spewed stuffing from its seats, had upholstery lining hanging down, and was missing its second gear.

"I've got this great record," he would tell his customers. "The Lord has really anointed these musicians. You've got to buy it."

"Well, we've never heard of it."

"Have you heard of Calvary Chapel?"

"Sort of. But look at those long-haired characters on the album cover."

"Listen, you've got to have this; it really relates to this generation."

"O.K., well, we'll take two of them."

"No, no, you need six. Can't you take six?"

"O.K., we'll take thirty-day credit."

"No, it's just cash on the barrel-head."

And they would buy it. Maranatha! Music quickly produced a second album, "Come to the Waters," by the Children of the Day. Record selling was hard work, and Michael was green at the business; but God was training him, teaching him, and grooming him. When his musical colleagues showed more interest in concert bookings, follow-up mail, and Bible correspondence courses than in distributing, Michael was encouraged to form his own distribution company, which he called Living Waters Pro-ductions. The results were astonishing. The little "com-pany" was soon doing a remarkable monthly business out of Michael's garage. Response to the two albums was twenty-five thousand copies sold during the first six months after their release.

As for the MacIntosh family salvage operation, the key word was "struggle." Michael labored under some early Franciscan conceit that he shouldn't take more than $150 a week from the record sales, that the rest was God's money and should be used to expand the ministry. That meant keeping the Valiant running on baling wire and chewing gum while Sandra scraped the cupboard bare. But despite the problems, it was a home transformed. Christ was now the head of the house; and instead of drugs, confrontations, and disappearances, there was joy and the laughter of children.

Little miracles were continually taking place. When there was nothing in the house to eat, Michael would be invited to conduct a Bible study, and someone would set a carton of groceries in the Valiant's rear seat. Or he would open his Bible and find a ten-dollar bill someone had slipped between the pages of the Book of Daniel. Once a whole ham was presented to him, and for a week Sandra was serving up baked ham, sliced ham, broiled ham, minced ham, and diced ham. The truth was that money no longer interested Michael. He was expecting the Lord Jesus to come back anytime, and what good would money be in heaven? Does God redeem sweepstakes tickets? Does a hearse carry a trailer hitch?

Meanwhile Calvary Chapel was in full stride, attracting international attention and gaining a reputation as the fulcrum of the Jesus Movement. Television crews were flying in from Holland, Britain, Italy, France, and Ger-many to record the spectacle. Reporters from national newsmagazines swarmed over the church grounds. The elders responded by erecting a tent to hold 2,200 additional seats.

For some time Michael had been hoping to be taken on the staff at Calvary Chapel as one of Chuck Smith's trainees for the ministry. To be a ministerial assistant, he felt, would give him the experience in direct evangelism for which he yearned; and his success with the records in no way deterred him from that goal. Much of his prayer time was spent in petitioning the throne of divine grace to allow him one day to become an evangelist.

One afternoon in March 1971, as he was talking over wedding arrangements with Pastor Chuck, Michael ventured to say, "I really feel that one day God is going to have me working with you."

Pastor Chuck looked at him the way a coach might look at a fourth-string quarterback. "Well, Mike, only time will tell."

But time went on ticking off the weeks and months and told nothing whatever while Michael's passion to preach the everlasting gospel remained unabated and unrealized.

Eventually Lonnie Frisbie, the young evangelist who had delivered the message the night Michael was converted and who later baptized Sandra, left Calvary Chapel to minister elsewhere. Once again Michael timidly approached his pastor. "Chuck, I know how busy you are, and I just want to help in any way. You have all these weeknight services. If I can teach or preach, let me know. I feel the Lord wanted me to say this, or I wouldn't be bothering with it."

The daring appeal left Michael limp, but Pastor Chuck was unflappable. "We'll pray about it," he said.

Pray about it! What did he think Michael had been doing? Instead of dispensing burglar alarms, Michael wanted to set off an alarm that would wake up all of

America, wake up the whole world. But nothing happened.

Three weeks later Pastor Chuck called Michael into his study and sprang the news: "Another young man has asked to become an evangelist, Mike. I'd like you to alternate with him for about eight weeks, and we'll see."

Michael was ecstatic. What a privilege, what an honor! Calvary Chapel was one of the great churches of the world, and here he was invited to teach in it. He went home to Sandra with the good news and spent hours boring into the Bible, preparing his messages. Wednesday came and two thousand people crowded the new tent.

Eight weeks later Michael's hopes were at the bottom of the gully. Wednesday night attendance had dropped. Fears and suspicions, the legacy of his paranoia, came back to haunt him. When Pastor Chuck walked into his little Living Waters Productions office, he expected the worst. But what Chuck said was, "Mike, the board has voted to take you and Tom Stipe and Don McClure on staff at seventy-five a week and give you a ninety-day trial to see if you fit into the ministry."

*You're kidding,* Michael thought. *Thank You, Jesus. I'm actually going to teach in this place. Wow. I can't believe it. All the odds were against it. My record, my lack of formal training, the drop in the crowds, everything; and here the breakthrough has come. It isn't possible. Hallelujah!*

He was so excited, he didn't even hear the mention of seventy-five dollars. His salary had just been halved.

# 21

# We Don't Ordain

*Do the Duty which lies nearest thee. Thy second Duty will already have become clearer.*
Thomas Carlyle, *Sartor Resartus*

Churches are traditionally run by boards that operate under the ancient law of the Medes and Persians, "which changeth not." Calvary Chapel's ministry, by contrast, was whatever Chuck Smith believed the Lord was leading him to do. That was how it came off. If you were in the flow, you belonged there; if you were drawn in a different direction, you moved on. The young assistants and staff people did what they were expected to do, without being privy to a lot of decision making and inner counsels. You want to know what to do? Seek God's will. Get in the flow, brother.

The months from April to December 1972 were critical for Michael as he received basic instruction in the care and feeding of Christians. Not that he was given a portfolio of duties connected with the services; he just slipped into them as one slips into a jacket. Thus he led the singing, prayed, preached, conducted meetings, gave invitations, and counseled seekers. He also planned concerts, made hospital calls, led the singles fellowship, answered the phone, pushed chairs around, and picked up cigarette butts on the church grounds. Always sensitive to the gaps in his education, he began acquiring commentaries on the Old and New Testaments and books on church history. He dipped into psychology and tried (seriously this time) to acquire some of the classics of literature. But study time was limited, for now he had a lively young family to support.

Chuck Smith was impressed. When he first met Michael, he was afraid the young man's use of hallucinogenic drugs had been so extensive that he would never regain a normal outlook. He had seen so many who had suffered severe personality damage and even brain damage. He soon discovered that Michael was a personable guy with a lot of drive and enthusiasm and love, but he also noticed a vagueness about him and an inability to stay on the subject, whatever it was, for any length of time. After Michael had been around for some months, however, his pastor noticed a change. The young convert began to show responsibility in the tasks assigned him. It also became obvious that he had ability. When Michael took over the distribution of the first Maranatha musical recordings (which Chuck Smith had personally advanced the money to produce), Chuck observed a young man not only with potential, but also with a willingness to get out and serve. His remarriage to Sandra stood very much in his favor. Michael was proving himself, making good moves and wise decisions.

As for Michael, his feeling at the time was that he wanted to be like Chuck. He recognized that the man was a prayer warrior and a great student of the Bible, and he made that his own goal. Chuck's love for and grasp of Scripture made Michael want that grasp. All his life, he felt, he had been a double-minded, insecure person with no backbone or purpose. Now he was beginning to accept the inspiration of the Bible and the responsibility and privilege of serving the Body of Christ. Love for the Lord Jesus Christ and respect for the Body of Christ, such as he had seen in Chuck, were ingrained in him.

During his eight months' apprenticeship Michael's speaking skills also developed. He showed the ability to communicate spiritual truth and season it with humor. Invitations came to speak at nearby high schools and colleges and occasionally to preach in churches. It was becoming clear to some, at least, that people were coming to Christ under his ministry.

The grapevine had it that after serving three months at Calvary Chapel a young assistant would be ordained a minister of the gospel; but in Michael's case the months sped by and nothing happened. Finally in September he mustered enough boldness to speak to Pastor Chuck: "People have been asking me to conduct their weddings, Chuck, and I was wondering..." To conduct a wedding, state law required ordination; but if Michael was expecting a formal ordination ceremony, with prayers and speeches and the gathering of relatives and the laying on of hands by visiting dignitaries, he was in for a shock. Calvary Chapel was a legally independent corporation, considered itself a New Testament church, and conducted its affairs accordingly. Pastor Chuck gave his assistant an application form. "Fill this out, Mike. To marry you have to be ordained. We'll take it to the board for action and see what happens."

Michael was excited. "You mean for ordination?"

Chuck shook his head. "We don't ordain anybody, Mike."

"Then what—"

"All we can do is ratify what the Holy Spirit has done."

But what did that mean? What had the Holy Spirit done? Who would sign the certificate? Did he expect God to sign it? Or was this just a religious way of saying it was the end of the line?

"You have already been ordained by God," Smith went on, and a hundred-pound sack fell off Michael's back. "We'll give you a piece of paper. That will authorize you to marry people. It will also get you into the jails."

In a few days the board voted its approval, making Michael Kirk MacIntosh an ordained minister of the gospel, a man of the cloth, a shepherd of the faithful, and a preacher of the Word of Life. But Pastor Smith did not even notify his assistant; the word came to him through Elder Bob Ward who had been present at the meeting. Eventually the piece of paper showed up. Chuck Smith was a most unceremonial gentleman, and he knew quite well how to keep the doorkeepers of the Lord's temple from waxing too proud.

# 22

# Honey vs.
# Cod Liver Oil

*I have measured out my life with coffee spoons.*
T. S. Eliot, "The Love Song of J. Alfred Prufrock"

Selah, Wing and a Prayer, Country Faith, Good News, Mustard Seed Faith, Blessed Hope, The Way, Love Song, Children of the Day—Calvary Chapel in 1972 was awash with such music groups, made up of long-haired, bearded, reclaimed sinners who were forever fooling around with their cables, lights, sound boxes, mikes, bass guitars, acoustic guitars, electric guitars, and traps. In time they formed a fraternity, an "in group" totally absorbed in what they were doing, and very noisy. When they were performing, people listened with fascination and applauded enthusiastically. When they were not, many of the same people tended to avoid them.

But not Michael; he loved the music-makers. The beat was in his bloodstream and these were his buddies, a part of his generation. He would pick up one of their guitars and strum the few basic chords he knew and be happy. The groups would cart him along in their vans to churches and campus meetings, and after their concert he would give his testimony: "Jesus saved me from bankruptcy...Jesus put my family back together...Jesus healed me from acid flashbacks."

Michael's affinity with the musicians had come to the attention of Pastor Chuck Smith back in the Living Waters days. Smith had incorporated Maranatha! Music in 1971, but after several months of sensational growth he sensed that the leadership of the company was taking it in directions with which he did not agree. He wanted to make a change, and he knew Michael had a vision that paralleled his own. They both thought the music money should be plowed back to help the musicians support themselves as they ministered in high schools and colleges and out on the beaches. So Smith dismissed the people who had been running the company and asked Michael to take over.

In January 1973 Michael was transferred from the church ministry proper and appointed pastor and director of Maranatha! Music. For the young pastor's assistant it meant leaving the church work he loved; yet it also meant that his salary was back up to $150 a week. He was again in the world of business; but this time it was God's ordaining, and he had a brand new challenge, a developing market and an exciting product.

In the next two years under Michael's leadership, the company was on its way to becoming one of the largest and most popular Christian record producers in the world, with an ASCAP label and a diversified line of products. Michael was not a detail man, and he could easily have fallen on his face had he not received expert help. His mentor at this period was Robert J. Ward, the man who had been president of the burglar alarm enterprise, who had since joined Chuck Smith at Calvary Chapel.

Six feet two inches tall, forty-two years old, an ex-Air Force pilot, blond, with a mind like a computer, Ward was now pastor of the new Maranatha Evangelical Association. This was Pastor Chuck's effort to respond to the dozens of communities in the United States and Canada that were writing and telephoning him, asking for help for their churches and even for Calvary Chapel ministries to be formed in their localities. Ward's efforts were restricted mainly to California and Arizona.

Before becoming a Christian, Ward had been a broker specializing in international finance. He took Michael under his wing and taught him the basic principles of business, of which Michael knew very little. He taught him to let his "yea" be "yea." If Michael entered a transaction, he learned to live by what he said. Ward taught him to plan and administer and be a good steward of God's money.

Ward also was used by God to help Michael mature so that he could grow out of all the psychological problems and irresponsibilities that had plagued him. He spent hours counseling with Michael, pointing him in the right direction, encouraging him. He became a big brother to Michael. Like Michael's older brother David, Ward had served in the Air Force in Korea and had flown missions as an F-86 pilot.

Ward also introduced Michael to a level of society he had never known. Many of the people he knew had position and wealth and knowledge of the world. So while the Holy Spirit used Chuck Smith to groom Michael spiritually and train him as a minister, Bob Ward was used to mature him as a man and as a communicator. If Smith's teaching on biblical prophecy expanded Michael's horizon of thinking, Ward's teaching on practical application helped him understand his environment.

Within a few weeks of assuming his new role, Michael found himself on a jetliner bound for the Philippine Islands with the Love Song musicians. This amazing turn of events came about through the ballooning popularity of Love Song, which was under contract to United Artists and had recorded three of the Philippines' top ten hits of 1972–73.

The invitation came from secular Filipino promoters, who featured the group at leading hotel supper clubs in Manila, at the University of the East, and on national television. Michael's chance came during five public concerts given by Love Song in Manila's Rizal Memorial Stadium, starting on Valentine's Day. Fifteen thousand people a night bought tickets and turned out, some smoking pot, some drinking beer, all there for the music. And each night Michael stepped to one of the microphones and gave his testimony of deliverance. When the invitation was then given to receive Christ, the response was incredible. By official estimate, during the five nights in the stadium, as many as seventeen thousand people came forward to put their trust in Jesus Christ as Savior and Lord.

Love Song was also the overwhelming attraction at the University of the East rally. Many people couldn't hear Michael's testimony because of all the yelling and screaming. President Marcos had recently declared martial law in the Philippines and had forbidden public meetings. This rally was the first exception granted, and national guardsmen in khaki uniforms were everywhere. They formed a human chain to get the performers through the crowd. The trip was a new kind of mind-expanding experience for Michael, because he saw vividly what God could do with evangelism. A seed was planted in Michael that God would water. A friend told him at the time, "I have a vision for China, Mike."

But all too soon midnight arrived, the ball ended, and the pumpkin coach flew the pastor of Maranatha! Music back to Cinderella's cottage. Instead of floating across the Pacific in a jetliner, he was bumping up U.S. 99 in a van to the cities of northern California—Sacramento, Marysville, Chico—and freezing with his musicians in places like Flagstaff, Arizona.

In April Michael rounded up sixty young people from Calvary Chapel, and they drove with the Maranatha musicians to Palm Springs in the lower California desert for a week of meetings. Each night the stands at the local ball park, known as Angel Stadium, were filled as five hundred persons showed up to hear the music; many received a touch from the Lord. During the day Michael sent witnessing teams roaming the city streets and school campuses, passing out leaflets that invited people to the Bible classes that were being held in the International Hotel and to the evening rallies. After the week of meetings closed, Michael and some of the musicians continued to drive into the desert for Saturday night services at the hotel. One night they were singing and having a good time in their hotel room when the manager called up. It seemed the plaster was falling off the ceiling into the cocktails of people in the lounge below.

"You'll have to move somewhere else."

"Where? We paid for this room!"

"O.K., tell you what. I'll put you out in the pool area."

That was the most fortuitous thing the manager could have done, because all his balconies opened up on the swimming pool, and the cocktail lounge adjoined it. When the musicians went into their beat, all the hotel guests came out on the balconies and listened to the songs about Jesus Christ. Barflies brought out their drinks, tourists filled the lawn chairs, and the gospel entertainers had a packed house without even looking for it. Then Michael stepped out and preached a gospel message.

It had its hilarious aspect, but the venture ended in frustration. The team had to move to another hotel, and the open door at Palm Springs seemed to be closing. Michael was forced to take stock of his situation. Where exactly was he? It seemed inevitable that after each taste of honey he would be handed a dose of cod liver oil. If he worked up an opportunity to preach, as likely as not the door would slam on him. If he put together a massive concert at Long Beach Municipal Auditorium, Tom Stipe or somebody else from Calvary Chapel would be assigned to deliver the main message. God had called him to preach the gospel and win souls, he knew that, but as the months went by he seemed to be doing mighty little of either. *I'll never amount to much*, he told himself. *I can't preach. I'm a lousy minister*. The effects of chemical excess, the drag of the wasted years, had not entirely disappeared.

When little Megan, the precious first fruit of the reunited marriage, was born in August of 1973, the growing family was still living on $150 a week, and Michael was still trying to level his mountain of debt. The demands of home were increasing. The business world was becoming more involved. Projects he tried to start came to nothing. Clients and customers either misunderstood him or took advantage of him. Personality clashes impeded the work. It seemed to Michael as if everything he did was wrong. He felt he was in God's way, and he wondered if He were trying to kill him.

Michael went back to spending more time in the Scriptures, relearning what the Psalms and the New Testament said about trusting, loving, forgiving, and taking the lowest place at the table. He realized that his traveling companions, the musicians, were not always as taken up with the things of the Lord as they were with their music. On their journeys in the van he began reading to them from the devotional writings of Andrew Murray, Charles Spurgeon, G. Campbell Morgan, and Norman Grubb. In Flagstaff, as he had done in Palm Springs, he divided the men into small units and had them on the downtown streets, passing out evangelistic tracts and handbills.

But his calling remained unfulfilled. Michael felt that promoting albums, paying out royalties, and putting together concerts was not what God had laid out for his future. During the closing months of 1973 he experienced what many a Christian had gone through before him—disheartenment. He was learning what it means to be crucified with Christ.

In a sermon on "Discouragement" which he delivered over a century ago, Charles Spurgeon told his London congregation, "Depression comes over me whenever the Lord is preparing a larger blessing for my ministry. The cloud is black before it breaks, and overshadows before it yields its deluge of mercy. The Lord is revealed in the backside of the desert, while his servant keeps the sheep and waits in solitary awe. The wilderness is the way to Canaan. Defeat prepares for victory. The raven is sent forth before the dove. The darkest hour of night precedes the dawn."

In Michael's case the preacher spoke prophetically. If God was bringing his servant to a Golgotha of spiritual death, it was because he was about to open the windows of heaven and pour out a divine blessing upon him. Something surprising and marvelous was already in the works.

# 23

# San Diego Welcome

*Others have labored, and you have*
*entered into their labors.*
John 4:38

America's prisoners of war were home at last from the nightmare of Hanoi. The fateful noose of Watergate was tightening around the White House. The first man to step on the moon was teaching college students in Cincinnati. Radical groups continued to spill animal blood over Pentagon files. Child pornography made its shocking appearance as a full-scale industry. Homosexuals held their first street parades. The drug culture was reaching down to fifth and sixth graders. Charles Colson announced his conversion to faith in Jesus Christ. Billy Graham preached to over a million people at one sitting in Seoul, Korea. The Jesus Movement emerged on the West Coast, surprising everyone—church people most of all.

It was October 1973. Steven Keeling, a young haberdasher in San Diego's Ocean Beach district, was looking for a change of direction in his life. His younger brother Dean, an Orange County landscaper, was attending services at Calvary Chapel in Costa Mesa and had given his heart to Jesus Christ. Dean telephoned Steven, and that's the way it all started.

The Keelings had grown up in San Bernardino, and while in high school they had indulged in the craze for hallucinogenic drugs and joined the counter-culture. Steven in particular took everything on the market short of heroin. Then in October 1970 he married and moved to San Diego, where at the age of twenty-one he opened the "Rare Comforts" clothing store. The store proved popular and things went well, but Steven was not happy with what he was seeing in San Diego. He had tapered off his drug taking, but his friends were increasing their use. Those who were married were pairing off with the wrong people. Some were in jail. Now twenty-three years old, Steven was in a receptive mood when his brother called and said he had been listening to some fantastic musical groups at a church in Costa Mesa.

On a Saturday evening Steven and his wife, Barbara, drove up I-5 to Calvary Chapel to hear the concert. After the musicians left the platform a young fellow came out to speak. His name was Greg Laurie, and he wore long hair and a beard. He told of his own personal involvement in the drug scene and how Jesus had cleaned up his act. The Keelings were deeply stirred by the message, and when Greg gave a gospel invitation to those who wished to receive Christ, Steven and Barbara were among those who crowded to the front.

Back in San Diego, excited for the first time about the Christian life and with the music of Calvary Chapel ringing in their ears, the Keelings began looking around for a church. But it seemed that services they attended were different. There was no beat, the hymns were unfamiliar and seemed old-fashioned, the announcements were interminable, and the preaching was more tedious than not. Where was the spirit they had witnessed in Costa Mesa's "gospel swamp"? Where was the exuberance, the spontaneity, the singing of fresh melodies, the strong meat of Scripture, the tiptoe excitement at the invitation? Where were the Spirit-filled worshipers spilling over with the love of Jesus?

The following week the Keelings drove back north, taking with them their shop assistant at the Ocean Beach store, Steve Ellingson, and his live-in girlfriend, Mary Wunderlich. At the close of the meeting Ellingson went forward and committed his life to Jesus Christ. Afterward they met brother Dean, who introduced them to a red-bearded giant of a carpenter and told them, "This is Don Abshere. Ask him to come down to San Diego—he'll teach you the Bible." Big Don grinned, and the next week he showed up. Seven people gathered that evening in the simply-furnished living room of Steve and Barbara Keeling in the Point Loma district. Two of them were from Orange County—Don and a painting contractor from Huntington Beach, Don Schock. The other five were the Keelings, Stephan Ellingson, Mary Wunderlich, and a young woman named Kathy Reilly. Kathy was a waitress who had dropped in at the Ocean Beach clothing store that afternoon as a shopper. Keeling had waited on her and invited her to his home.

So they had a Bible study, and Kathy Reilly was saved. Like that.

At the moment Michael MacIntosh was a hundred miles away, feeding his baby daughter and feeling perplexed about problems at Maranatha! Music. It is safe to assume that San Diego was the last thing on his mind.

By February of 1974 the weekly Wednesday night Bible study had expanded somewhat. Steve Ellingson and his girlfriend were dissatisfied with their living arrangement. Both were under conviction of the Holy Spirit, and decided to break up housekeeping. Mary, a Christian who had fallen away, had renewed her faith that night at Calvary Chapel. She moved into an apartment. Steve also tried the celibate life, but it seemed to lack something. One night after going carefully into the Bible's teachings on the subject he hit upon what seemed an admirable solution—marriage! It evidently qualified for the Bible's sanction and seemed to hold a lot more promise than the single life. The Keelings agreed with his conclusion.

But now a new problem arose: who would tie the knot? It had to be a Christian, that was certain. But Chuck Smith was too far away, and the local clergy were distant for their own reasons. Ellingson's hair hung down to his shoulders. Don Abshere had a suggestion: "I've just moved in behind a friend in Tustin named Mike MacIntosh. He's on staff at Calvary Chapel. I think he can do it. I'll ask him…."

"All the way down there for a wedding? I don't have the gas money, Don," Michael said.

"We can scrape it together, I think."

"But don't they have any preachers in San Diego?"

"It's a personal favor to me, Mike."

The wedding took place in February 1974 in the Keelings' living room, glowing and fragrant with azaleas and carnations fresh from an Ocean Beach florist. The bride looked sweetly triumphant and the groom had his hair cut—slightly. Michael, rather starchy in gray suit, white shirt, and tie, read the service, preached the gospel, and pronounced them man and wife. All went nicely until it was found that some unwelcome guest had spiked the brownies with marijuana. As the officiating clergyman, Michael had barely made it to Point Loma on an empty gas tank. When he was ready to depart for Orange County, the gas stations were closed and he had to siphon his fuel out of another vehicle in the wedding party.

Welcome to San Diego, Michael MacIntosh. And come back soon.

# 24

# Favor and Flak

*You therefore must endure hardship*
*as a good soldier of Christ Jesus.*
2 Timothy 2:3

But Michael didn't want any part of San Diego.

Why not? Don Abshere wanted to know. He was becoming restless. The long drive to Point Loma was irksome. Some Orange County musical groups were asking for Don. The Keelings on the other hand needed someone to take over the Bible study.

No, thanks. All of Michael's interests, his home, his family, his work, his friends, his church, and his future were in Orange County. Maranatha! Music was expanding all over the place. There were problems, but nothing that San Diego could help solve. It was too far away, and the group was small. Let someone else do it.

Michael was putting in a lot of time on the road with the musical groups, traveling as far north as Washington state. On weekends he was teaching big Bible classes in Palm Springs. To add San Diego to his itinerary would mean that his young and growing family would lose out on a daddy already away too much.

Yet the appeals from San Diego were insistent. Attendance was growing. Would he help organize a church? No. Not now. But he would pray about it.

Finally, in June 1974, Michael capitulated and told Abshere, "All right. God has been on me about this. I'll drive down and teach the Gospel of Mark on Monday nights. Sixteen chapters, sixteen weeks. Then I'm coming back to Orange County to stay. O.K.?"

The first group met for study in the Keelings' home, and 12 people showed up. Monday was not a good night. But by the time Michael reached the tenth chapter of the Gospel of Mark, the number had swelled to 75, almost all being under twenty-five years of age. He decided to experiment. After a Maranatha! Music concert he often felt frustrated because the testimony time, when he was supposed to speak, was so brief. Some of the San Diegans had been asking about the musicians; and he decided to bring them south, not for a concert, but to provide musical highlights to a Bible study. This would avoid the stigma of "gospel entertainment." So Point Loma Junior High's auditorium was rented, and 150 people showed up; another similar event was held the following week, and 300 turned out. Then on the next Monday evening 90 people jammed the Keeling living room to hear not music, but the thirteenth chapter of Mark.

Obviously it was time to move. Accommodations were found in Balboa Park's Hospitality House, where there was seating for five hundred. Michael finished teaching the Gospel of Mark, but no way could he stop. He opened the Book of Revelation, and each week the crowds increased as the word spread. Here was a young guy who had something. He was saying that Jesus was more than a carpenter and was describing what the Bible had to say about the way things were going. He had a terrific sense of humor. The music was out of this world. Everything about it was captivating. God was doing something unique in San Diego! And they turned out in Balboa Park by the hundreds.

And yet the offerings barely paid for the gas from Orange County and a burrito and Coke for the teacher.

A fairly convincing sign of divine approval in evangelistic work is the rise of opposition. One Monday night when Michael was about to start preaching from Revelation in Hospitality House, Don Abshere (who decided to come back to San Diego) whispered to him, "The ushers tell me a man sitting in the back row has a .45 calibre pistol in his waistband. I've called the police." In a very short time four police officers quietly entered the room where the meeting was being held. While Michael kept on explaining about the seven vials and the plague of hail, one of the officers leaned over the shoulder of the armed man and snatched the pistol out of his belt, after which the man was escorted from the room. Perhaps a dozen people noticed the incident.

At one Hospitality House gathering a man high on "speed" began uttering loud curses at Michael. When the ever-vigilant Abshere asked him to leave, he refused. Don then picked up the man bodily and carried him out of the room, while his charge jerked at the red beard and walrus moustache. But after he got him well out of earshot, Abshere set his man down and talked to him about Jesus.

One time Abshere, Michael, and Don Schock were driving from Costa Mesa to San Diego in a Dodge Maxivan, singing songs about Jesus, quoting verses, and thinking about how God had been blessing His own work. In four months, attendance had jumped from 12 to 150. That night they had rented Point Loma Junior High's auditorium for a special rally and anticipated a packed meeting. As they passed the San Onofre nuclear plant a highway patrol car cut across the divider and began following them. Soon a second patrol car drew abreast of them and then slowed after making eyeball contact. By the time they reached Del Mar two other patrolmen were following them, one on a motorcycle. Red lights began to flash and sirens to wail. After Michael, who was driving, pulled over, a loudspeaker barked, "All right, you in the green van, I want hands in the air." And four officers leaped out with shotguns.

Michael glanced in the side-view mirror and saw that the motorcycle policeman had his pistol pointed at his head. Again the speaker barked: "All right, I want the passenger in the front seat to get out first." That was Don Schock. He found himself facing one of the shotguns. "O.K., now we want the driver out." But Michael's seat belt was fastened. How could he keep his hands up, unfasten his seat belt, and get out of the car? The pistol was still pointed at him. Only two weeks earlier a driver involved in a Newport Beach holdup had his head blasted off by a police officer who thought the man was reaching for his gun when he was unarmed.

"Get out of the car, driver!" the loudspeaker repeated.

"I've got my seat belt on!" yelled Michael, as Abshere tried to explain his dilemma to the officers.

"O.K., we want the other passenger out." Abshere got out, after which an officer approached the driver's side, kicked the door open, and said, "All right, take your seat belt off, but keep your hands where I can see them. Then reach for the glove box and get me your I.D. and everything else in there." Michael obeyed, keeping one hand in the air, and was then escorted with the others to the rear of the van, where the officers surrounded them and began holstering their guns. They were smiling.

"What's this all about?" demanded Michael. They still had their hands on a squad car.

"Mistaken identity. Four guys in a green van just like yours robbed a tire store back there in Dana Point, and we had an alert that they were headed this way. You fit the description, long hair and all that. We figured the fourth guy was lying in the back with the money and the tires he stole; and as soon as we came up, he would jump up and start shooting. We're really sorry."

"Are you kidding?" said Michael indignantly, pulling out his ordination card. "You could have blown my head off!"

That night Michael related the incident to several hundred people gathered at the rally in the Junior High auditorium. He added, "You never know. I pointed out to one of the officers the sticker we had on our back window. It said very plainly, JESUS IS LORD. I told him I thought that might have tipped them off that we were O.K., but he replied they had been fooled that way before!"

# 25

# The Meeting

*Prove Me now in this....If I will not open for you the windows of heaven and pour out for you such blessing that there will not be room enough to receive it.*
Malachi 3:10

"Apply yourself to the whole text, and apply the whole text to yourself," wrote Johann Albrecht Bengel, the eighteenth century German biblical scholar; and as 1974 drew to a close, Michael MacIntosh was doing just that. The more he taught in the Book of Revelation, the more he felt the beginning of judgment upon himself. It seemed that God was doing things inside him, that he was being brought to a place to die and see himself crucified with Christ. Three times he had tried to leave the work at Maranatha! Music because of internal problems, and each time Chuck Smith had told him, "Pray about it." But there comes a time when prayer alone doesn't seem to work, when something has to be done. "A time for every purpose under the heaven," Scripture reads (Eccl. 3:1). But when does that time come? And how do you know?

The Monday evening crowds in Hospitality House were growing restless. They wanted a church. They had rented a house in San Diego's Ocean Beach and put an army cot in it for Michael. By now Michael was spending two nights a week in San Diego, and a spirit of revival was in the air—a spirit that was all the more frustrating because of the turmoil back at the ranch. On Monday evenings six or seven hundred people were crowding the Hospitality House, and people were coming to Christ by the dozen. By November, the Ocean Beach Women's Club had been rented in order to start a Sunday morning service, and some forty persons began attending. Counseling was taking more and more time, and just finding a place to talk was not easy. The Ocean Beach house was a tiny cottage, and the benches in Balboa Park, which they were sometimes forced to use, were subject to interruption.

"What would you think," Michael said to Sandra one day, "if we were to move to San Diego?"

Sandra was pregnant with their fourth child and in no mood to move. But she was also aware of what Michael had been going through. She saw him being pulled two ways and sometimes three or four, and she was praying for him daily. She knew that Michael was still living with conflicts from his early life and that while there had been a lot of healing, it was only the grace of God that sustained him. She felt Michael had turned into a wonderful father. The man who had once told her he was relinquishing all rights to his children now would die for any one of them. She loved him for it. He was spending time with them, telling them Bible stories, doing things with them, even confessing his sins to them, saying, "I haven't been home enough; I haven't disciplined you guys enough. Let's all pray and ask the Lord to forgive us." She liked the fact that Michael was an exciting person to be around; he had a zillion ideas and was off in a new direction every day. Being conservative by nature, she thrived on it. But she also knew she could be happy anywhere with him.

"I know God is doing something in San Diego," she told

him, "but I hate to leave here. It would be an awful wrench. But I'll go wherever you go. If you told me we were moving to Australia, I would start to pack and give God the glory."

The solution to the problem, obviously, was a meeting with Chuck Smith. For five years he had been Michael's pastor, counselor, instructor, guide, and visible seat of ultimate authority. After fortifying himself with prayer and the encouragement and support of Sandra, Michael went to the pastor's office. He was prepared to submit his resignation, but hoped he could stay on through the Christmas holidays so he would be able to buy the children some presents. He felt he had failed miserably, that Chuck Smith disapproved of his handling of the Maranatha! Music company, that his mistakes of judgment and commitment were irretrievable.

But what Pastor Chuck said to him was, "Mike, how would you like to move to San Diego?"

Michael blinked and shook his head. "Do you mean it, Chuck?"

"Of course I mean it. And we'll give you a month's paid vacation starting now, so you can begin there the first of the year."

It seemed that Chuck felt Michael had magnified the problems at Maranatha! Music out of proportion and misinterpreted how he felt about them. While Michael thought he had failed, he didn't realize that Chuck had been watching what was happening in San Diego and had become convinced by the Spirit of God that San Diego was ready, and Michael was the one to be there. He knew God was going to bless Michael and the ministry in San Diego.

Chuck stepped over to where Michael was sitting, and laid his hand on him, and prayed, committing him to the new work and to the care of his heavenly Father. And Michael, who thought he was "right with the Lord" but in

Dutch everywhere else, was suddenly handed a ministry that he had never sought, never wanted, and never expected; and he sat in the pastor's study and bawled like a baby. For it was quite evident that God had never intended anything else.

# 26

# New Watchword on the Marquee

*Behold I will build me a nest on the greatness of God.*
Sidney Lanier, "The Marshes of Glynn"

Some people call San Diego "the good Los Angeles,"
with its palm trees, its magnificent harbor, its smog-free
air and balmy climate. Others call it sleepy, laid-back, the
northern tip of Mexico; they claim the rest of California
hardly knows it is there. But when Michael MacIntosh
drove his little Volkswagen south and planted his flag in
San Diego in January 1975, "America's finest city" (as it
calls itself) was growing like a weed and approaching a
metropolitan population of one million. Tijuana, a few
miles to the south, was growing even faster.

Michael's first move was to schedule Sunday morning
worship services in the Hospitality House. These quickly
went to two services, while the Monday evening Bible
studies were still drawing hundreds of listeners. The need
for larger facilities was immediate. Michael found a realtor who had bought an abandoned church building and
was trying to rent it. The congregation on Linda Vista Avenue had dissolved in bankruptcy. The property had two
auditoriums, one of which had been used to hold a Bible
school. Michael rented the smaller one, and on the first

Sunday in February 150 people showed up for morning worship. By Easter the congregation had swelled to 650 at two services.

But Sundays were only part of the excitement. The Monday night Bible studies began drawing crowds running from 1,200 to 1,300. The church only held 750 seats; and people were camped on window ledges, in the foyer, and wherever they could be squeezed in. The Bible study was moved to Wednesday night, which caused a temporary drop in attendance, but soon the crowds were larger than ever. The worship services were a blending of traditional elements, of features borrowed from Calvary Chapel, and of the MacIntosh touch. There were no song books, no choir, no piano or organ. The old hymns and gospel songs were sung occasionally; but the worshipers seemed to prefer new melodies, many of which they were writing themselves, melodies that expressed their love and freedom in the Lord. Usually a guitarist would lead the singing.

The media woke up to the fact that the ministry of Calvary Chapel (as it was called) had become the talk of the religious community. People spoke of the "anointing of the Spirit"; they said, "Jesus is doing something in this city." Ministers showed up to study the worship order. Reporters wrote articles for the local press. Photographs were taken. Michael was invited on television talk shows.

The church began to take form. MacIntosh was the pastor, Don Abshere the assistant pastor. Dean Keeling had moved down from Huntington Beach and was putting together the Sunday school. Pastor Chuck Smith appeared to give his blessing to the newest Calvary Chapel. Both auditoriums were now in full use.

In April, Jonathan, the second child of the remarriage, was born, and six weeks later Sandra and her young family moved at last from Orange County to Escondido. By this time a thousand people were attending Sunday services at Linda Vista, and the walls of the old church were beginning to bulge. College students, young married couples, and people of different ethnic backgrounds came, listened, and joined. Michael was counseling people every day, often from 9 A.M. until 7 P.M.

One evening Scott Gehrman and his wife, Charlene, walked into the church. Scott considered himself a quintessential child of his culture, a long-haired, dope-smoking, pill-swallowing, draft-dodging, pilfering, sex-turned-on rebel whose bitter grievance against life began at age thirteen when his mother died. His father, alarmed by the boy's aberrant behavior, ordered him to talk to a minister. Scott's response was to disappear from home for four days. As he grew older the rebellious streak became more sophisticated. Marriage did little to tame it; his philandering continued. Charlene, however, began attending the Linda Vista church and met some friends who soon looked up Scott and invited him to the services. "It's not a church like you think of church," they assured him. "We even have rock concerts!"

Scott finally decided to go and get it over with. But the minute he stepped inside the building, he sensed something different. Looking around the packed auditorium, he saw blue jeans, long hair, and people his own age. Unpleasant memories of past church experiences faded away. The singing began, and at first he couldn't tell where it was coming from. Then he realized it was coming from the people. Excitement was in the air. When Michael MacIntosh appeared, he was wearing jeans, a T-shirt, and tennis shoes and carried an open Bible and talked about love. The longer he spoke, the more Scott related to him. An invitation was given, and Scott Gehrman responded. As he opened his heart to Jesus Christ, the gall of bitterness that had poisoned his life for so many years seemed to dissolve. The pain of the empty years was dropped into the sea of forgetfulness. The man was healed.

But the Linda Vista site still was not the answer for a church blessed with rapid growth; so when 1976 arrived, Calvary Chapel was once again on the quest for new quarters where there would be room to keep on growing. In June of that year Michael and Sandra attended a showing of the World Wide Pictures classic, *The Hiding Place*, at the North Park theater in San Diego. As Michael looked around the vast interior with its seating for 1,200 persons, he whispered to Sandra, "What a great home this would make for us!"

Sandra looked at the rococo decorations around the stage and whispered, "Maybe."

"I mean, this is what we've been looking for!"

"I'm watching the movie."

"But don't you see? I wonder what they want for it!"

"Shhhh."

Within a month Michael was having a conversation with a realtor friend when the latter remarked, "I've got an old theater for sale."

"Which one?"

"The old North Park theater on University Avenue."

"I'm interested. What's the down payment?"

"Seventy thousand dollars."

The combined Sunday morning and evening services at the Linda Vista site now totaled close to two thousand. Few churches if any in San Diego County could match that figure. The rented facilities were obviously outgrown. But the idea of a building campaign, with high-powered fund-raising activities, repelled Michael. He decided that if the worshipers at Calvary Chapel wanted North Park theater (which had recently begun running X-rated movies) as a permanent place of worship, they would have to provide the money. He would take no special offering.

The money came in and the theater was bought. The ornate old theater with its tired decor was refurbished top to bottom. The orchestra pit was entombed under wooden planks, the drops and curtains were raised, the floors recarpeted. The stage on which vaudevillians like Ted Lewis, Sophie Tucker, and Burns and Allen used to hoof it while spieling their songs and monologues was opened up and made a platform for musicians and preachers. The marquee out front that used to advertise *Gone with the Wind* and *High Noon* now announced GOD LOVES YOU!

In less than three years from the time Kathy Reilly was saved in the Point Loma living room of Steven and Barbara Keeling, the miracle church had found a home. From that living room to the Junior High auditorium to Hospitality House to Ocean Beach Women's Club to Linda Vista to North Park theater, the story was one of God's bountiful increase. And the end was not yet.

# 27

# Lupines and Poppies

*And the Lord added to the church daily*
*those who were being saved.*
Acts 2:47

By the early the 1980s, Calvary Chapel in San Diego had become one of the largest churches in the city, passing five thousand worshipers through its doors each week. Its Sunday school was teaching the Bible to fifteen hundred children and youths.

A magazine, *Horizon*, had been started and was reaching out with a lively gospel message adapted especially for readers in their twenties and thirties and picking up national journalistic awards. A nine-month school of evangelism was training hundreds for full-time evangelistic ministry.

A radio and television outreach was growing rapidly. A military ministry was sending out literature, Bible study tapes, and videotapes to naval personnel aboard ships and to servicemen's wives' groups. A hospitality ministry was feeding four hundred senior citizens twice each month at a "King's supper."

Home fellowship groups were meeting weekly in a hundred homes throughout the county. A new million-dollar education and family center, across the street from the place of worship, housed a variety of Christian activities. There were ministries to women, music lovers, prisoners, people off the street, individuals with personal problems.

But what if the growth continued? Was it destined to become another gigantic superchurch? Michael turned to the Scriptures for guidance and learned that nowhere did the early apostles specialize in attracting crowds or erecting buildings. Instead he found this word from the apostle Paul to young Timothy: "The things that you have heard from me among many witnesses, commit these to faithful men who will be able to teach others also" (2 Tim. 2:2). In other words, don't accumulate—proliferate!

Michael had already gathered together a remarkable team of qualified young men, many of whom had received training under Chuck Smith in Costa Mesa and had followed Michael to San Diego. Now it seemed that the Spirit of God was moving them out. Edward Smith, who once was master of Mansion Messiah and now was assisting his former deacon, began gathering a congregation near the ocean front at Encinitas. Don Schock went to Chula Vista on the Mexican border; Ray Bentley went east to his homctown of El Cajon; Glen Gundert went to Point Loma, Peter Mallinger to El Centro in the Imperial Valley, Jim Hesterly to Poway, Don Abshere to Escondido, Ron Spineto to Alpine, David Riley to La Mesa. Calvary Chapels were springing up like lupines and poppies after the California rain.

For a new church to be formed in a rapidly growing area like southern California is not unusual. The difference was that the people who made up these new congregations were, for the most part, young and had not been going to church. They weren't aware that churches existed that taught God's Word and exalted Jesus Christ and at the same time made them feel comfortable without expecting them to alter their appearance.

Let's assume it is one of those heavenly Sunday mornings in San Diego when earthly sin seems to slink out of sight. Palm fronds are waving in the sea breezes under the canopy of an ultramarine sky. We approach the old North Park theater on University Avenue and learn that Michael MacIntosh is preaching this morning. Hundreds of casually dressed young people are beginning to cluster on the sidewalk under the marquee. We follow them through the doors into the sloping auditorium, and as we find a seat next to some friendly people, we notice that the stage is occupied by a solitary young man perched on a stool and holding a guitar. The ancient, massive theater organ has been still for years.

The seats are filling up fast as soft singing commences.

> We have come into His house
>     to call upon His name and worship Him.
> Let's forget about ourselves
>     and concentrate on Him
>     and worship Him.[1]

The singing goes on, not for ten minutes but for forty or more. Sometimes the worshipers clap in time; sometimes they lift their hands in adoration. The mood continues:

> And Jesus said,
> Come to the water, stand by My side.
> I know you are thirsty; you won't be denied.
> I felt every teardrop when in darkness you cried,

---

[1] "We Have Come into His House" by Bruce Ballinger. © Copyright 1976 Sound III, Inc. Used by permission only. All rights reserved.

And I strove to remind you that for those
tears I died.[2]

After a while an associate pastor appears and speaks a
brief word. Then an offering is taken. Now Michael Mac-
Intosh in slacks and open shirt steps to the podium. Opening his Bible, he begins to speak in a pleasant, rapid voice.
His words flow gracefully, his vocabulary is vivid and
descriptive. His subject matter is a passage from the
Bible, but he swings easily from the first century to the
twentieth. Occasionally there is spontaneous applause
and even laughter, but the message is a serious one that
touches upon suffering, evil, and judgment. Forty minutes later Michael is inviting people to give themselves to
God and surrender their lives to His Son, Jesus Christ.
The audience begins to stir. Couples, singles, people of
every age, runaways, long-haired, short-haired, prosti-
tutes, drug addicts, all are streaming toward the front.
Counselors join them, and the business of the kingdom
goes on. Older persons are frequently seen among the inquirers, for the young in heart will not be denied what
they missed in their past.

Now the congregation disperses, for another crowd has
gathered on the sidewalk outside, and in the evening the
auditorium will be filled again. And all week long the
church's ministry will continue in prayer meetings, training classes, counseling sessions, team huddles, and home
gatherings.

Gary Priest was a trainer of whales in San Diego. His
exciting work took him not only around the pools at Sea
World on the back of Shamu, but all around the United
States and Canada on radio and television promotional

tours. Ten years earlier Gary and his wife, Kathy, had been married in a Christian ceremony, but since then they had elbowed Jesus Christ out of their busy schedule. Kathy was a professional hair stylist, and one day a member of her exclusive clientele spoke to her about the love of Christ and invited her to a service in the North Park theater. Gary joined her. It did not take them long to recognize that they were listening to a different beat. "When we saw the love Christ has for His church shining through Pastor Mike, it lighted up our lives as well." One sad note darkened their marriage: three years of fertility tests and ten years of married life convinced Gary and Kathy that they would have no children. But then they found a verse in 1 Samuel: "Those who honor Me I will honor" (2:30). It doesn't always happen, but it did for them. A year after their own renewal of faith they were bringing their baby son, Austin, to the front of the theater for dedication to the Lord.

All this in San Diego, a vacation city that is supposed to be far more interested in football, baseball, dune buggies, eating, surfing, beaches, and boats than in God.

# 28

# The Moving upon the Waters

*O earth, earth, earth,*
*Hear the word of the LORD!*
Jeremiah 22:29

Shortly after Michael and Sandra remarried, during their days in Tustin, Michael came out of the apartment one morning to find a girl he knew, who sometimes acted as their babysitter, crying. She was standing by a car with the trunk open, while behind her were two men with cocktail glasses in their hands. Michael recognized one of them as an auto wholesaler —a ripoff artist and a drunk. The other man was fat and wore a Buddha necklace.

"What's going on?" Michael demanded.

The fat man spoke up. "She threw a Coke bottle at our car and cut the tire. We're making her fix it."

By this time the girl had lifted out the jack and was carrying it to the front where the tire was flat.

"What did they do to you?" Michael asked her.

"Made fun of me. Whistled at me. Tried to proposition me."

Michael took the jack away from her, but the fat man came toward him. "Get out of here. She's going to do this."

Michael jacked up the car and began removing the tire. "She is not going to do this. Where's the spare?"

"Got no spare. She has to fix it."

Michael stood up, went to his car, and removed the spare tire. He brought it over and put it on the wheel.

"You don't have to do this," said the wholesaler.

"Get the money from her for your tire," said the fat man.

"You keep the tire and get out of here. I don't ever want to see you again," said Michael. At that the two men closed in on him. He stood, the tire iron in his hand, and the old MacIntosh was flaring, but he caught himself. When he spoke it was in a quiet tone: "Don't pull anything on me. I rebuke you in the name of Jesus Christ." The moment passed and the men drove off.

Michael invited the girl to Calvary Chapel where she soon became a Christian. But a few months later she was tragically caught in a traffic accident on Pacific Coast Highway at Corona del Mar. Her small sports car was crushed and her body badly mangled. As it happened, a friend of Michael's was horseback riding near the highway when the accident occurred, and he rushed to the scene. Seeing her condition and realizing that there was nothing he could do, and being a Christian but not knowing who she was, he asked her if she knew God.

"Yes," she whispered, "but please pray for me because I haven't been doing too well with Him." He prayed with her, and she nodded her desire to give her heart afresh to her Lord. Before other help could arrive, she died.

That incident played a central part in changing Michael's attitude toward his fellow human beings. The weeping girl, soon to die, became for him the exemplar and personification of every defenseless and needy human being on the planet. She taught him his role. Instead of using a pretty woman as he had done in the past, he had defended her. Instead of taking his own part as in all his fights, he had taken someone else's. He saw now what God wanted him to do with the rest of his life, and later found it confirmed in Scripture: "Open your mouth for the speechless....Open your mouth, judge righteously, And plead the cause of the poor and needy" (Prov. 31:8–9).

When Michael made his first trip to Asia in 1973, he met that man who had said to him, "I have a vision for China, Mike." He was "Brother David," an ex-Marine living in Manila who found Jesus Christ at Billy Graham's 1969 Anaheim Crusade in California. His friendship with Michael ripened, and in the spring of 1976 he invited Michael to go with him on a fact-finding mission to the Chinese borders. For Michael, the heart of the three-week journey was a five-day visit to Burma, where missionaries have long been forbidden but where Christianity is thriving in spite of repression. In Rangoon the full gamut of human misery and wretchedness met his eyes. As he walked down the main street he was overwhelmed by the sight of deterioration, the boarded-up banks and principal buildings, the soot, the apparent lack of human initiative and desire to alleviate the poverty and distress everywhere evident. He remembered the text: "...plead the cause of the poor and needy" (Prov. 31:9).

A main business in Rangoon was to deliver one hundred Burmese Bibles to the Baptist church. Michael was given the role of carrying the suitcase of Bibles down the stairs of the Strand hotel to a taxi. The cab turned out to be a 1941 English Austin. Michael spotted it out the window, then looked down at the hotel restaurant kitchen just as three rats, each the size of a cat, ran into it. He reached the street level and saw two Burmese wearing sunglasses, reading newspapers and watching him. He hurried out to the taxi, followed by the pair, and got in the cab, which refused to start. Eventually the driver took a crank from under the seat and got it started with a snort and a bang. They arrived at the Baptist church with the electrical circuit on fire and smoke coming out the rear. Two minutes after the Bibles were delivered to the waiting Burmese pastors, they were hidden. Among the Karen Baptists of Burma the ratio is twenty-five Christians for each Bible.

The real challenge of the trip, China, was presented to the little party of four after they flew north along the Irrawaddy river to the romantic—but poverty-ridden—city of Mandalay. Here they had established a rendezvous with a Chinese pastor who had walked for two days from the People's Republic to meet with them. The man made a permanent impression on Michael, who saw in him a symbol of a billion people. Forty years old, the pastor had been imprisoned by the Red Guards during the "cultural revolution." A huge scar on his face was caused by the butt end of a rifle. He was, however, a difficult prisoner, as one jailer and a number of cellmates were converted to Christ during his internment. Now released from confinement, he was the founder of nearly a thousand Christian fellowships.

With more than two dozen people gathered in a house, which was really a hut, on the main street of Mandalay, Michael was asked to share his Christian testimony. Lookouts were posted on the street while he spoke. When the Chinese pastor learned about his deliverance from the use of drugs, he inquired about the extent of the drug traffic in America. His home was close to the "golden triangle" where much of the world's opium is grown. Michael told him the nature of America's problem, and the pastor replied, "Please tell the people of America that the young people in China who love the Lord Jesus Christ are praying for the young people in your country who have drug problems." And Michael thought, *I wonder how many young people in America are praying for the young people of China?*

Michael flew back to America with a fresh vision for his

ministry. He determined to establish a school in San Diego where people would be trained "to serve God in a purposeful ministry somewhere in the world." The Lord gave him a name for this exciting venture—The San Diego School of Evangelism. But the more he thought about it, the less he wanted it to become a conventional Bible institute. Rather, it would take a person already somewhat grounded in the Bible and put him or her into active service for the Lord.

And now was the time to act! The angel was moving upon the surface of the waters, the end was near, and many millions were waiting to know the saving, renewing, healing love of God in Jesus Christ.

# 29

# A New Vision

*Write the vision and make it plain on tablets, that he may run who reads it.*

Habakkuk 2:2

The San Diego School of Evangelism opened its doors in the fall of 1976 and was an immediate success. Classes were taught on the top floor of the offices once used by the North Park theater management. Neal Pirolo, a former missionary to Brazil who had been a school principal under Chuck Smith at Costa Mesa, became the director. Pirolo's educational background and bent for cross-cultural evangelism yielded dramatic results. After his students were trained he wasted no time in sending them to the far corners of the world, where they learned (often the hard way) what it is like to communicate the gospel in an indifferent environment. Pirolo built his curriculum upon intensive Bible teaching, church history, history of missions, language study, comparative religions, apologetics, evangelistic methods, media training, and—always—practical experience. Pirolo himself traveled extensively throughout the world, searching out locations where his students could effectively serve the Lord with at least some community support.

The "practicums," or periods of service, varied according to the local need. Thus in Israel some students worked in a kibbutz on the Golan Heights; in Australia they taught Scripture in local schools of New South Wales, engaged in youth work at Koala Park, and passed out tracts in Sydney's Kings Cross district. In Holland they mixed with "internationals" in youth shelters. In Hooper Bay, Alaska, they lived and worked among the Eskimos. In Hailsham, England, they formed a church and visited prisons and schools. Other areas to which their practicums have taken them have included Hong Kong, Macao, Korea, Jordan, the Philippines, Hawaii, and Canada. When Billy Graham conducted evangelistic crusades in the western states and western Canada, scores of students from the School of Evangelism traveled to serve as volunteers at the events. Sacramento, Tacoma, Spokane, Las Vegas, and Edmonton were visited.

In 1982 the school acquired a new director, Dennis Magnuson, and under his leadership some remarkable new chapters are being written in the history of missions. Magnuson has designed the practicums as a sifting process whereby the church can discern which of its members are called by God to full-time evangelistic service. The students continue to help out at evangelistic crusades in many capacities and to go abroad to cross-cultural spheres of action, but Magnuson has also introduced them to the wilderness. In some of the loneliest spots of the west—the Sierra Nevada mountains, the hills of Santa Catalina Island, Death Valley—the students are tested in a natural environment. They learn to live with God and each other; and while the scenery is magnificent, the training is often rugged.

One element that has characterized the School of Evangelism from the beginning has been its insistence on instruction in sound biblical doctrine. Both day and evening classes are immersed in the Word of God. A qualified faculty has provided teaching that (according to the testimony of some students) compares favorably with the instructional level of America's most reputable universities. Among other subjects, the students are exposed to New Testament Greek as well as to modern languages.

When Michael MacIntosh was invited to Mexico City to conduct a series of evangelistic meetings, Magnuson arranged for the series to be included in one of his School of Evangelism's field trips. Thirty-five students arrived in the Mexican capital from Tehuacan, where they had been working with churches and youth groups and conducting meetings. They made their headquarters a warehouse that had been purchased by a former School of Evangelism student. This man, John Lilley, came to Christ under Michael's ministry while he was obtaining his master's degree in business administration at San Diego State University. He then moved to Mexico, applied for Mexican citizenship, and changed his name to Juan Domingo.

The warehouse became the site of Horizon's crusade in the spring of 1984. It served also as kitchen and sleeping quarters for the American visitors and as the locale of all-night prayer vigils. Meanwhile all kinds of interesting things were happening in the city. The evangelism students had not only learned to speak Spanish, they had written and rehearsed a street drama, which they presented several times during the week. The plot involved a confused young woman who was tempted by demons, and then encountered Jesus of Nazareth. The acting was lively, the drama was moving, and the response enthusiastic. One day the students presented their play on the plaza of the Basilica of Santa Maria de Guadalupe in the religious heart of the capital.

Another evangelistic tool that proved effective was a clown act. Five students put on full makeup and appeared in a city park as clowns, quickly gathering a crowd with their acrobatics, juggling acts, comical antics, and jokes. Children particularly were attracted, and it was not long before one of the clowns was telling the small ones about Jesus. While the parents looked on indulgently, he led some thirty youngsters in a simple prayer of commitment. And all the while, other students were handing out leaflets announcing the crusade services in the warehouse.

Michael's preaching, with Juan Domingo's interpreting, concentrated on Bible themes. It was well received by the Mexican people, and each night some fifty or more persons came forward at the closing invitation to profess or renew faith in the Lord Jesus Christ. Both before and after the message the musical team from San Diego played and sang, and seemed to offer exactly what the listeners wanted. It was Christian, contemporary, tuneful, happy, and loud.

By the end of the week of meetings the crowds had increased to three hundred, and people were asking why a church should not be formed. Several months later Juan Domingo was teaching a weekly Bible class attended by thirty-five persons and preaching on Friday evenings to a crowd of 150 Mexicans. Once there was an empty warehouse; now there was a church. "[You] once were not a people," Peter wrote to the twelve tribes scattered among the nations, "but are now the people of God" (1 Pet. 2:10).

It wasn't always so smooth. When Michael first conceived of the School of Evangelism, he thought of it as an instrument to touch the world for Christ, not as an institution with deep roots in a particular place. As pastor of a church, he could see that the school, and in fact the whole pastoral ministry, involved duties and responsibilities that God required, but that he, Michael, did not feel called to discharge. Details of church and school organization, he felt, could be carried out by others more gifted and better suited to the tasks. In order to avoid getting his priorities out of order and neglecting his family, he put together a team and turned over some responsibilities to young men and women he trusted. The result was that he made some mistakes.

The first major mistake was to send a team of eleven people—seven women and four men—to Thailand for six months. Invited by an elderly Chinese couple whom Michael had met in 1976 and who wished to retire from a fruitful ministry, the team was expected to take over the operation of a Christian orphanage outside of Bangkok and eventually a Bible school as well. But the team deviated from Michael's original plan and confusion and embarrassment resulted. Feelings were hurt. Established missionaries in Thailand misinterpreted Michael's motives and became upset. Michael assessed it as "one of the most excruciatingly painful episodes of my life." He was forced to make an air journey across the Pacific and apologize to people all the way from Singapore to Bangkok to Hong Kong, and subsequently faced a rift in his own congregation.

As is usually the case in such situations, the problem boiled down to a very few people who were disaffected and unhappy with the pastor's direction. It took months to work out, but eventually the unhappy ones left and healing took place. But Michael learned a painful lesson: never again would he send a team so large to any one place for so long a time without mature and dedicated leadership.

In November 1981, Michael and sixteen of his church leaders spent four days and nights in the Anza-Borrego desert, waiting on the Lord for the direction of their ministry. One midnight as they were praying, God seemed to impart to them a fresh inspiration. It was time for them to take a fresh step, to move into new paths. The procedure became clear: they were to win, disciple, and send, and their evangelism would involve all three elements. The name "Calvary Chapel" would be changed to "Horizon Christian Fellowship," which would in turn become part of Horizon International Ministries, a worldwide evangelistic enterprise.

The design for this whole ministry Michael found clearly laid out in the first chapter of the Book of Acts: "You shall receive power when the Holy Spirit has come upon you; and you shall be witnesses to Me in Jerusalem, and in all Judea and Samaria, and to the end of the earth" (v. 8).

Horizon Christian Fellowship, the church in which Michael was ministering, was to be Jerusalem.

He was to labor in the Spirit to make the people who came to North Park theater into strong Christians who would walk in the Lord, would know His Word, and would bring in others to help who had gifts of ministry.

Judea would be San Diego County. He was to work together with other Christians and local churches in the Body of Christ to present the whole county with the gospel through evangelism and teaching. He was to see that churches were planted where they were needed and then train people to lead them, without taking anything for granted.

Samaria would be the United States of America, its territories and possessions. Michael had always loved his country, which he now recognized as a gift of God. Now he added a desire to reach his country for Christ through the medium of mass communication. As doors opened, he was to use literature, radio, television, and evangelistic crusades.

The "end of the earth" meant for him the world, the

habitable portion of the planet, which from now on would be laid on his heart as a field to be reached with the gospel of Jesus Christ.

Once the vision became clear, new churches were soon gathered and are now flourishing under local leadership not only in San Diego County, but in Hawaii, Mexico, England, and other places as a result of the groundwork laid by Horizon people. And yet there seems to be no parochial spirit in this enterprise, no allegiance to a doctrine narrower than the whole New Testament. Like the early followers of the "poor man of Assisi," these new-style missionaries are going about their religiously fragmented planet making friends and talking about Jesus, who was a friend of people. They aim to compete with no one and to love everybody. They create no denominational enclaves and keep no conversion graphs. In many cases they are not "sent" at all; they simply go. Home ties to Horizon Fellowship are extremely loose. They go as members of the Body of Christ, as people who love Jesus and desire to share that love, with a motivation much like that of similar movements in the past—the Brethren of the Common Life, the Quakers, and most notably the young Galilean disciples of Jesus. Most refreshing of all is the fact that they are not taking bureaucratic administrative positions, typing up reports in a mission compound or teaching English in a girls' school. Not that such works are not worthy and holy in God's sight; but these people prefer to be out on the street, like Paul and Barnabas in Lystra and like Adoniram Judson in Rangoon, making contact with the public, handing out leaflets, and inviting one and all to a Bible meeting.

When they come home they may leave behind a church of Bible believers gathered from street and high-rise, or they may not; but they erect no compounds and put up no steeples. They are simply singing a new song.

# 30

# Into the World

*Go, and catch a falling star.*
John Donne, "Song"

In the spring of 1978, something for which Michael had prayed and yearned and worked ever since the fledgling days at Mansion Messiah came into being. He received a call from Anglican Canon James Wong of Singapore, inviting him to preach the gospel at public rallies and to address a convocation of believers. The call marked the beginning of his ministry as an itinerant international evangelist.

As pastor of Horizon Christian Fellowship of San Diego, Michael had never concealed from his congregation the tug of the regions beyond or the conviction that God wanted him to extend a hand of love to the whole world. In the years that followed that first trip to Singapore he received invitations to conduct preaching missions and to speak at rallies in many countries, including Sweden, England, Scotland, Hungary, Poland, Hong Kong, the Philippines, Thailand, Mexico, Nicaragua, and other nations of Central America. In addition to public appearances in these countries (in 1984 over one thousand Latin American men and women responded to Michael's invitations), he met with evangelical Christians in Switzerland, France, Denmark, East and West Germany, Czechoslovakia, Uganda, Austria, Romania, and the People's Republic of China. In 1982 he knelt in prayer with the persecuted "Siberian seven" in the basement of the American Embassy in Moscow, where they had been living for nearly five years. The people of Horizon Christian Fellowship sent truckload after truckload of food and medical supplies into Poland and Uganda, and in some cases Michael was the driver.

Michael was invited to take part in Billy Graham's 1983 Conference for Itinerant Evangelists in Amsterdam, Holland, and to lead a workshop on how to give an evangelistic invitation. He has visited with Dr. Graham, has traveled with members of his team, and has no illusions about the glamour of such a ministry. As one who has emerged from a culture and time-period different from that of the Billy Graham crusaders, Michael brings a different emphasis, a different style, and a different set of interests. Yet the message of the gospel of Jesus Christ is the same—just as the message Michael heard at Calvary Chapel, Costa Mesa, was the same one he heard as a boy in

Portland's Montavilla Baptist Church.

As he begins his forties and looks down the road ahead, Michael says, "I want to erect not buildings, but men and women who will stay on fire for the Lord their whole lives. If they are single, I hope they will catch the vision and the zeal, and go and serve the Lord. If they marry, I hope their partners will have the same zeal and vision they have. I have just so much energy. I want to use it in a people-centered ministry. If there is a change coming in evangelism, I want to be part of it. To get hold of key people, to motivate them, to send them out—that's the goal. I would like to see every church involved in sending people out to do evangelism, not just supporting parachurch organizations that do the job for them."

How does Sandra feel about all this? She says, "I am called to be Michael's wife, and that's what I am, no matter what he does. I will function in whatever capacity God leads Michael to. When Michael travels, as he does, then I miss him. But as Ruth Graham said about Billy, I'd rather have him part time than any other man in the world full time. Michael and I have no wonder-working formula. We are just like everybody else. Michael's success and anointing as a minister almost stops when he comes in the door. He is just the same husband and father that everybody else is. It is God who provides the miracle ingredient, and my chief concern is that the glory goes to God." Sandra's parents, the Riddets, by the way, have become Christians and are among Michael's enthusiastic prayer partners.

Pastor Chuck Smith was once asked his opinion about the future of Michael MacIntosh. "Mike," he said, "is a visionary. He has a vision for the world. I really believe there will be fellowships all over the world, led by people who have gone through his school of evangelism, and who have been inspired for the ministry *and are just out doing it!* I see it as touching the world, without any limitation on it at all."

Much of Michael's story has been sad—he was a young man whose path kept taking him downhill, and he belonged to an eager but distracted generation that often could not find itself. But his and Sandra's is a tale with a happy ending, and it may well be in the providence of God that the best is yet to come. Five vivacious children (Phillip was born in 1979) are growing up in a home in Poway, California, that seemed at one time to be smashed to pieces. Now, by a miracle of grace through the Lord Jesus Christ, it rings with praise and laughter. And so, by the same grace, does many another home.

# Epilogue

Emerson wrote that men are what their mothers made them, and undoubtedly Ruth Lane Osborn was for many years the strongest influence in Michael's life. To him she was a beautiful woman who was doing her best in an unfair and unequal world. He loved her dearly, appreciated her, and felt sorry for her. Every time he or his brother took part in a high school wrestling match or track meet or football game, she was there. How she got off work he never knew. "She worked so hard," he says. "She sacrificed and sacrificed. She did all she could to be a mother and a father and a provider. I could see it. And sometimes Kent and I would try to clean up the house and do the dishes and put a cup of coffee on. Even as a little boy I would walk a mile to the bus stop to meet her with an umbrella. We were very close. We three were all we had in life. It was as if we joined hands together and said, 'No matter what, we're going to make it through.' "

But Michael also saw that his mother hindered herself because of a lack of self-confidence. He hated being poor. It seemed the rent was too high for her income, and the bill collectors were always coming around. In later years life became easier for Ruth. She became the "girl Friday" in the office of the Associated General Contractors in Eugene and was prominent in the "Women In Construction" organization, serving first as regional and then as national director. When colleges in the Pacific Northwest held "career days" for their students, Ruth would be invited to speak on the woman's role in construction. When the contractors association held a banquet, they would have Ruth address them. They liked her knowledge of the industry and they liked her humor.

Ruth was living near her mother in Eugene in the spring of 1970 when a letter arrived from Michael, addressed to his grandmother. He knew that Grandmother Ella had heartily disapproved of his earlier behavior and had blocked his effort to enroll at the University of Oregon by refusing a loan. This, however, was a missive of peace. He told her that he loved Jesus and had become a Christian, and he had to clear up his relationship with her. He also told her that, as her grandson, he was going to become the minister she had always wanted one of her own sons to be. He said that he loved her very much. Ruth and Kent sat listening to Ella as she read the letter to them, and they couldn't believe it. When Ella finished and remarked, "Isn't that beautiful?" they thought otherwise.

"It's just another thing," said Ruth. "He's gone crazy on some new subject."

"She's right," agreed Kent. "It's another cult."

"I think it's disgusting," added Ruth. "I liked him better when he was into the flying saucers. That was exciting."

What bothered Ruth most were the memories Michael's letter aroused in her. Twenty times she must have gone to the altar as a child, attending Nazarene revivals in the Dakotas. "My guilty conscience sent me up. Even if I didn't have anything to be guilty about, I still went," she explained to Michael. She knew that for more than half a century her mother had been praying for her, and she resented it.

In the early spring of 1971, Ruth was astonished to receive an engraved invitation to the second wedding of Sandra and Michael. She couldn't believe it. Again the reaction: "Mike is crazy!" She couldn't imagine why he would make a second run at it when the first one had failed. It was certainly something she would never have attempted. So it was one of those things, and the ceremony in Costa Mesa's Calvary Chapel went off without the mother of the bridegroom being present.

Two months later Michael tried again and invited his mother to take her first look at her grandson, who was now two years old. The little boy was named not only after her firstborn, Michael's half-brother David, but also after her own father. This time she couldn't resist, and took a week's vacation from work and flew south. While she was visiting the family, Michael invited her to Calvary Chapel to hear Chuck Smith at a Sunday morning service. She expected Chuck to appear wearing an iridescent, shiny suit and pointy-toed shoes. *Standard gear*, she thought, *for ripping off a bunch of kids*. When she took her seat, she found him in shiny clothes all right—a blue serge suit he had been wearing, it seemed, for about twenty-five years. He also seemed to have humility, and another quality she could not define. She listened to him.

The next day Michael asked her to accompany him to a Christian commune where he was to conduct a Bible study. But when she observed him going out the door barefoot, in jeans and T-shirt and carrying a Bible, she decided the evening would not be too illuminating. *This boy has a few things to learn about public speaking*, she thought. *I'll have a word with him afterward*. Then the music began, and they sang songs that they knew and she didn't. After a while Michael began to teach. His lesson was from Paul's letter to the Philippians. She looked around at the rapt expressions on the faces of the young men and women. Then she watched her son and was amazed to see a kind of glow on his face as he talked about the love of Jesus. She didn't think he knew the Bible at all, but he did. He clearly knew what he was talking about, and he held her spellbound. She looked at him, looked around at those kids, and whispered a prayer, "Lord, I don't know what he's got, but that's what I want!"

It was the turning point in her life. She was fifty-eight years old, and spiritually she had been her mother's despair most of that time, but now her hour had struck. She knew thoroughly what she had to do—she had gone through it enough times as a child. Before she retired that night, Michael came into her room and asked if he could pray with her. "That's neat," she said. But for the first time in a long while she cried. And after her son left, she made her peace with God and turned her life over to Jesus. It was a firm and permanent commitment.

But she didn't tell her mother, and she didn't tell Michael. As she later told Michael, "The old, wretched, phony pride that was always getting in the way of what I really wanted to do and be was hard to break." Only after she returned to Oregon did she call Michael on the telephone and tell him that she had taken Christ into her heart forever and now wanted to live a truly Christian life.

Michael's reply stayed with her: "Mom, I knew it all the time!"

Eventually Ella learned what had happened to her daughter, not verbally, but by her actions. Ruth began to pray with her. And when Ella ended her pilgrimage in 1972 at the age of eighty-two, Michael flew north to conduct her funeral, it being his first. He also found a church where he felt his mother would be welcomed and feel at home. She united with the church and worshiped there until she retired and moved to San Diego, where she became active in organizing women's intercessory prayer groups and helping in the office at Horizon Christian Fellowship.

Ruth Osborn's hair is white now, but her vitality is undiminished and her chuckle is as catching as ever. As for her Christian testimony, it remains virtually what it was back in 1971: "As soon as I saw what the Lord did for Mike, that was for me." But her spirit has been taken over by a greater Spirit, and God has made the difference. "When I sit in church and listen to Mike's preaching," she says, "he is not my son; he is my pastor. I don't take any credit for that. It belongs to the Lord."

To learn more about how to walk with Jesus Christ, or to receive further information about the ministry of Mike MacIntosh and his team, write to:

HORIZON INTERNATIONAL MINISTRIES
P.O. Box 28429
San Diego, CA 92128
(619) 487-0457

# Postscript

Many changes have occurred during the seven momentous years since this volume first appeared. On the personal side, two losses should be noted, as both are mentioned in these pages. William Riddet, Michael's beloved father-in-law, has left us for a better land. So has my wife of forty-six years, Winola. The church has moved itself to a new location, and now occupies a 20-acre junior high school campus in San Diego's Clairemont district. It has erected a new $1,500,000 auditorium-gymnasium in which two crowded services are held on Sunday mornings, and nearly-full services on Saturday and Sunday evenings.

Even the Clairemont move is proving inadequate as the congregation continues to expand. Horizon is now considered the largest church in San Diego County, and is featured in a new study as one of ten of the most "innovative" churches in the United States. Scores of young men and women have been trained in the Horizon School of Evangelism and have gone out to plant and lead churches throughout California and in many parts of the world.

Michael's ministry at Horizon continues to prove popular, both with the "baby-boomer generation" and with the younger set. He seems to understand the end-of-century young people and their problems better than most, having experienced them himself. He has become president of Youth Development, Inc., a Christian ministry founded by Jim Vaus, which operates one of the world's largest networks of youth crisis counseling. Doors have opened for him to embark on a national radio ministry, and the voice of Horizon is now heard in many major metropolitan areas from Honolulu to Boston.

Horizon International Ministries has developed a year-round program which faithfully carries out the original vision conceived back in the seventies. instead of conducting "crusades", Horizon has begun developing on different continents a "Festival of Life" concept which combines the evangelistic preaching of the Gospel with special ministries through medical teams, construction teams, competitive sports, outreach to prisoners, clown ministries to children, music, parades, training schools for Christian workers, and luncheon banquets with civic leaders. These have already proved highly successful in the Philippines and and Mexico, and Grenada is the next projected site.

Michael himself has added scholastic goals to his busy agenda, and has been awarded the master of divinity degree by Azusa Pacific University. He is currently a doctoral candidate at Fuller Theological Seminary. Michael wears the badge of chaplain to the San Diego Police force. His elder daughter, Melinda, is a recent bride and her husband, David Love, is pursuing an internship program on the Horizon campus with a view of future ministry.

Much more could be said, but this is a mid-stride report, with hoped-for greater things to come as God continues to bless Horizon. Eighty Home Fellowships are now meeting weekly throughout the county and are developing their own programs of neighborhood ministry. In all this growth the note of joy is still sounding clear on campus; prayer remains the church staff's highest priority; Satan is still being battled on every front, and week by week souls are being won to Jesus Christ for eternity. To God be the glory!

—Sherwood Eliot Wirt